Ungreed

Also from EATMS Productions

Books on power, survival, women's autonomy, and the systems shaping modern America.

Nonfiction

Billionaires, Capitalism, and Power

Evil and the Mountain Ungreed
Self Help for American Billionaires
Selfish Steve and the Ivory Tower
Tariffs, Taxes, & Face-Eating Leopards
Ban Billionaires: Fascism Fix

Fascism, Religion, and Cultural Control

Self Help for the Manosphere
Fascism 2025
Fascism & the Perverts & the Greed Virus
Christian Fascism Marriage Book
Tyranny, Table Manners, & Tiramisu

Guides for Women's Autonomy and Protection

How to Survive in Post-America as a Woman
Project 2025 American Drag
4B – Burn, Ban, Boycott, Build
4B OG – So No Go GYN
I'm Glad He's Dead

Analysis of Authoritarian Project 2025

Project 2025: The Blueprint
Project 2025: The List
Project 2025, Christian Dumb Dumbs, & The Republican Agenda
Fascism, Project 2025, & The Pinkprint

Modern Rewrites for Women

Stoic Principles Reimagined
Siddhartha Reimagined
The Prince Reimagined for Women
The Art of War Reimagined for Women
The Jungle Reimagined
The Constitution Reimagined for Women

Machine Learning Series

AI, Bitcoin, Nostr for Women
AI, Safety, & Security for Women
AI, Anxiety, & Health for Women
AI, Kids, & Family Safety for Women
AI, Creativity, & Personal Expression for Women
AI, Independent Work, & Parallel Power for Women

Social Systems Series

Emotional Labor for Women
Household Power for Women
Workplace Power for Women
Medical Bias for Women
Aging Systems for Women
Recovery Systems for Women

Fiction

Dystopian Stories of Resistance and Collapse

Propaganda Paige & the Missing Prosperity
Propaganda Paige & the TIDE Manifesto
Propaganda Paige & the Shadow Cartographers
Propaganda Paige & the Prosperity Alliance
Propaganda Paige & the Shattered Truth
Propaganda Paige & the Rising TIDE
Propaganda Paige & the Last Bastion
Propaganda Paige & the Dawn of Prosperity
Project 2025: Dorian — The Last Men
Project 2025: Boy — A Last Men Novel

Evil and the Mountain

Ungreed

by
Esme Mees

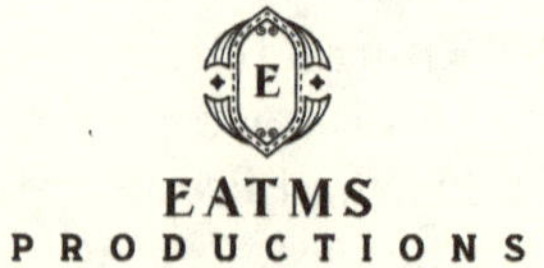

This title is part of an ongoing body of work. All EATMS Productions titles, across all series, authors, and formats, are components of a single connected project.

ISBN: 978-1-966014-03-4

Cover, interior design, interior prints by: Esme Mees

eatms@pm.me
www.eatms.me

Printed in the United States of America.

I care about you.
And I don't even know you.
-said no one
of great power and wealth
anywhere
ever

Preface

Being nice and rational with evil assholes doesn't work. Their brains are literally wired differently. They are motivated by disgust and fear vs. empathy and curiosity. What follows is a compilation of Socratic dialogues around their greed and Pie.

A system based on assholism aka market fanaticism, er, fundamentalism, is innately tied to an individualist ideology, to the belief that one's prosperity reflects one's worth, and therefore that any means of accumulation, including exploitation, is acceptable. Obscene excess in the face of terrible hunger and pain is justified.

A breakdown is coming, brought about by evil ass corruption. The carnivorous risks taken by ideological, financial, political, and religious institutions for the sake of profit will push the exploited masses to the point of demanding change. Those systems, upon which nations are built, and which foster great power and wealth at the expense of its citizenry are composed of persons themselves of great power and wealth. These individuals are evil and a virus to be eradicated. A moral mandate is laid down. Immunity sought; Pie is just such the thing for lasting ungreed- the antidote.

While those with great power and wealth are busy traumatizing the masses, already exhausted from dealing with ongoing pain and collective world suffering, a plan was hatched and is being carried out this very moment. Move in closely and listen for the clues. The cure to greed is with us. Pie. Pie. My dear sweet Pie. A slice for you. A slice for me. Good Pie, in the mind's eye.

Esme Mees, Winter 2024

Prologue

Professor- Why can't you be more genteel?

Pupil- That's right.

P- You remember it was that exact word, genteel?

p- That's right.

P- And you felt?

p- Like not being genteel.

P- What did you say back?

p- I think I yelled something not very genteel.

P- And?

p- Nothing.

P- Then what?

p- I slammed the door. Locked the door. And turned up the music.

P- What happened next?

p- Nothing.

Dialogue 1

P- And what of the statement- Nobody in power is coming to help the powerless. What follows?

p- On an individual level or as a whole?

P- Does it matter?

p- The sum of all parts, it matters.

P- If there is weakness, where does it begin?

p- In the individual or as a whole?

P- Does it matter?

p- The sum of all parts matter.

P- What of the system where they both reside?

p- If there is weakness in one, the many are not strong, and the system is weak.

P- Where does strength arise?

p- Empirically?

P- And what do you have besides your eyes, ears, and all senses that inform?

p- Well, then I see strength structurally arising from great power and wealth, but it is cosmetic. This is a strength we are told is strength by those with great power and wealth, a circle jerk. I hear of great suffering from my friends, neighbors, local community, and world community and am told by those with great power and wealth that their suffering, their weakness, is their own. Come to be that way by choices they made, but really, does anyone choose suffering if pleasure is nearby? I know I would not. Not for myself and not for others, for that would make one a monster.

P- And do your other senses tell you that is just the way it must be, that the weak are of one design and those of great power and wealth are by another design?

p- A system is composed of many from one. Great power and wealth for a few come from many. To leave behind your fellow human is to further a system where we are separate from each other. Where the whole is fragmented with cracks of suffering. The whole is then weak, not strong. Great power and wealth are an illusion. I taste this in my mouth as bitterness spews from the top blaming the bottom for not doing more to help themselves. And from the bottom, the hundreds of millions with empty bellies, hungry mama and thirsty babies spitting up sour stomach acid instead of settled by sweet milk.

P- Have you always had enough to eat?

p- No.

P- Was this a choice?

p- It is a false dichotomy. In that moment, of course not but where does the moment that leads to fullness begin? Should I have studied a practical art or science to secure greater wealth? Should I have learned to hunt and trap animals to secure food if I am without wealth to buy it? Should I train myself not to insist on so much sustenance that my grumbling stomach be trained not to make noise, not to make trouble for the rest, for if someone hears my stomach's plea, they might offer me food and it is not their problem anyway.

P- If it is not their problem and you are hungry, therefore weak, how is the whole to be strong?

p- But it's not strong because I am sometimes hungry.

P- Can you not choose from this moment, right now, to end the hunger?

p- In this moment I am sad I ever was hungry, afraid of being hungry again, and scared of where the hunger will lead.

P- If I have food and my belly is full would you have me share my food with you?

p- If you are of great power and wealth why wouldn't you share your food with me?

P- Because it is mine, not yours. I earned it. I am smarter, faster, and better than you. And if I am not of great power and wealth?

p- Then I am told by those of great power and wealth, as I smell their scent of fine wine, clothing, and privilege that you better not share with me because then you will have less. It is hard to ignore the smell and sparkle of a freshly baked pie though. Especially when they flaunt and feign that it is just a pie but also the best Pie.

P- And on my way to becoming one of great power and wealth, will having kept all the Pie to myself make me stronger?

p- But also weak because I am still hungry and there are more of us than you. If you are not careful, as they have not been careful around hungry eyes, ears, and bellies, their castle will not stand.

P- They have more food than you. Does that not mean they are stronger than all those that are hungry?

p- That's not right. All of us that are hungry are more than the few that are not. We have more numbers. We have more power. We are as strong as that Pie. All Pie.

P- You are not. They still have all the wealth. And now they want all the Pie and will use their great power and wealth to control as much Pie as possible. Though it must be for something amazing, the reason for their insatiable accumulation must of course be for some great reason. A purpose to account for why they are entitled to their doctored entitlements, such as their great power and wealth is a byproduct of manipulating the system in gimme form so that all benefit goes to them. They must perform miracles to warrant expecting to be treated like gods and saviors instead of monsters and vermin. What do they use their wealth on?

p- War and things. Destruction of souls, beauty, and nature. It is all a tautology acted out by vampires and goblins. Where does it end but for where I began, and you continue? Without blood or brains to dare or care until Pie came along.

P- Tell me about the Pie. What kind of Pie is it? The one they tell you is not big enough for everyone. Is it an illness, the wanting of not just more but the whole pie so much they are working on ways to leave this planet to get more?

p- Yes, sickos. It's flavor is part of the mind's eye of Pie. This is a beautiful thing about Pie. Pie is a new technology that plays on old senses. One where the meek are deserving. Initially, Pie's greed factor was a clever motivator. As the price for one whole Pie got bigger, people realized they would get less of what is known as finite Pie but more infinite Pie all around. They'll often enact riskier and riskier behavior to get more Pie. In the end, those that see Pie as more than just a new system game, the greater their benefit in service of Pie as form vs. function. Pie is much bigger than function. That has been a limiting dialogue around Pie.

2

P- Are you a destroyer or creator?

p- I. We. We are not destroyers. I will not destroy for profit. Unlike them. Those with great power and wealth, paid for by industry, tell me I am wrong in this. They lie. They do not gain if they do not lie. No value comes from these lies, only loss.

P- Is the lack of truth a weapon or a bruise?

p- Pie is for the delicate and indelicate alike. It is comprised of sharp angles. Math as hard protocol. Unforgiven mistakes. Value lost to you whilst rejoining the chain to be someone else's property, better idea. It is hard for the sensitive. We crave things that we are allergic to. Consume that which is too bad, too much. We over do. This Pie, at root, does not care that you are sensitive. It does not care what you believe. It will shape what you believe in time.

It's participants become bountiful hosts for it to grow. It requires cultivation by many. The few sensitive souls that have found and nurtured it had great financial motivation in the beginning. Still do today but since that part of it becomes less and less each day, as the slice size intimidates the bigger it gets, it is necessary to baby the little slices, the crumbs, as a message greater than one whole Pie. Most of us will never have a whole one.

This whole Pie my Pie should no longer be a point to admire or encourage. For if through slow kind care, through all of us working together, we break the old mold and enter the complete transference of one system for another. A more holistic, organic, and peaceful one, then the system itself will morph and change and become other. Dreamt in the dark to see the day, someday soon.

3

P- Will they ever tell the truth?

p- I read what is supposed to be the book of the century and it is awful. They use truth as an inverted weapon, we are the bullets.

P- Do they have small minds?

p- The small minds are coming to inflict more pain. They come due to their wounds. And hate, delivered as anger, mockery, and vice. Enacting laws. Getting away with evil. Themselves, often the embodiment of that which they seek to destroy.

P- How many times did you go crazy?

p- Technically, only once. Pretty regularly before, and daily after. Once you have lost your mind it is easier to stay on its edge. Almost as if pushing too far away is no longer where you belong. You don't dare stay there in the middle of the chaos pit lest you never return. It makes more sense there, feels too natural.

The small minds are coming to inflict more pain. They come due. Demanding compliance and servitude, what they think they are due. Due to their wounds. And hate, delivered as anger, mockery, and vice. Enacting laws. Getting away with evil. Themselves, often the embodiment of that which they seek to destroy. The whole lot of them are hair trigger hypocrites of self-hate and loathing so foul they dribble it on us like doddering endings, near dead souls, trying to spread the shame that eats them inside top to bottom down. I don't want your evil spell on me. Say it back to them. I don't want your evil spell on me. Give it back and stay far away, for they are sick with the curse of greed.

P- The part that keeps you from surrendering to it fully is worth knowing. Will does not seem a name for it. Survival does not seem a name for it. Centering does not work. Nor balance. The lack of attachment to a purpose must make for a difficult world to know balance. I am sorry you straddle these plains. I say this out of a natural and cultivated empathy where not belonging is uncomfortable. More so, it is frowned upon. Even condemned. It is deviant behavior to not fit in. To question one's place.

There was a time, for the leisure few not set to laborious task by feudal lords, whereby exploration of self and the universe writ large was encouraged. Encountered by those privileged, in effect to be on holiday, from moneyed making for their masters toiling, to seek for and from the pot of discovery. To find meaning was allowed. Not so today. Even oddness is illegal in some places.

These were a few moments, from a far, for a few, to be sure. For much of our time has been in service of the lords continued insatiable feed need for great power and wealth. Only come by through domination, it is only a wonder they have employed such simple modes of control. Opioids of religion, law, and actual opioids, and opioid like supposed sustenance givers, transgressive results imprisoning you in cycles.

For this cycle is clear. What do you now know/ own to be true?

p- The value of Pie.

P- What is it worth?

p- Bigger than a map.

4

P- Where is the loudest voice?

p- Not here. Out there. I don't want to do this. I sat on the sidelines hoping anybody would stand up and say the truth. I'm tired of the gaslighting. If I don't do it, and you, who will?

P- It will not be a lonely road for there are many who want the suffering to end. Will those with great power and wealth suffer?

p- Like an inverse funnel there is only up or down. The masses must squeeze their way to the top to outnumber the greedy evil doers that psychopathically aim to own it all. They will not be satisfied until feudalism is returned. Until we wear collars to keep control, it is just them vs. us. Pie is a tunnel we run to and through. Pie provides a mechanism to forge compromise based on the informed consent of the governed. I hear them say this, that, it will all be sorted out, after we destroy that distraction over there that we are desperate you fall for instead of realizing we are full of shit and distraction only gives us more time to rob you, beat you, and teach you how to rob and beat whoever standing next to you is the made-up scapegoat today. And then back to their crying game of yeah, maybe things will get better, someday, by whom? When? Does nobody stand up anymore? Will anybody tell the truth? Would we believe them?

P- Anymore implies they once did. There is always a tomorrow for when problems will be addressed and there is always a yesterday to compare that day to. After thousands of years, despite progression of a kind there is always an excuse for why progress for all must be delayed by the few. Given this is the natural, standard, state of affairs, who are you to question the order of things?

p- Who am I not to? Who are they to tell us this is just the way it has always been?

P- They are in charge don't forget. They won't. They won't let you forget they have great wealth and power, therefore they set the rules. Are you a rule breaker?

p- If the rules are dumb and wrong, who am I not to be?

P- They have set up a vast deterrent system of punishment and oppression for those that do not conform. It has worked for these thousands of years. They appear to have everything at their disposal to stop you. To not even bother teaching you a lesson because you are small. Instead, in the name of keeping it all together, yet it is really just like dealing with a knot with no thumbs. They squash, maim, and kill their opponents. You are not even as amusing as a gadfly to them. You are small and easily controlled. Their system functions well, as designed. Their tactics are inhuman because you are not human. If you are not in service of them, you are against them. That does not stand. Remember, this is their way for thousands of years. For hundreds of reigns. In many languages. With all the colors of all their customs, the end result is always the same. The story does not change. It does not die with you. The system keeps their story on a loop. As in days past, will their force and cruelty not stop you?

p- It is spiraling tighter, their story. The narrative is slipping and there is nothing left to lose. When they have stripped you of your dignity, of your humanity, only two paths remain. Creation over preservation. Preservation over destruction. Creation vs. destruction. An initiation from one level to a higher level joining fellow members of humanity.

P- The youth and disenfranchised must be incorporated?

p- And when I had the escape hatch, I wasn't fine because things were not fine. When you treat aspirations as achievements, you go off the rails. We have not achieved the possible, yet. It's not how Pie, it's why Pie. We will cradle and nurture it, for progress is not permanent.

5

P- Do they have too much power and wealth to go away?

p- For now, yes.

P- What should we do with them?

p- Shame them. As they have done, do with the insane.

P- Shame the insane, those with great power and wealth?

p- I don't have anything else to offer.

P- Is that true?

p- Unless I am in service of them.

P- And?

p- And the machine.

P- How do you stop the machine?

p- You break it.

P- How?

p- You interrupt it's system.

P- How it operates?

p- Yes.

P- How do you do that if you have no great power or wealth?

p- I don't know.

P- Don't you know a lot?

p- I know I am not them and do not want to be them, yet I am told I am to aspire to their height.

P- Yes?
p- That is what I am told.

P- Yes?

p- But it's not what I feel.

P- And that is?

p- Weak and powerful, both, at the same time.

P- Isn't that a lot to feel?

p- Yes.

P- Isn't that a lot to know?

p- Yes.

P- So then you are powerful?

p- Yes. And also, weak.

P- Where does the weakness come from?

p- Listening to them.

P- Can you stop hearing them?

p- I can turn them off. But not all the time.

P- Can you make them not so loud?

p- Yes.

P- If you have no great power or wealth, where does your power come from?

p- I know they are wrong. I know there must be another way to be. We cannot amass and achieve only to destroy and then foster suffering so easily. So casually. They know. Yet, they choose to do worse than nothing. They tell you it's your fault, that the system is fine and great and that the problems, mine, and ours, are all in our head. I think they want us to go insane. I think they want us tired, weak, and impotent. I think they are afraid that we know their ruse. I think they are running out of time, and it is the only thing they cannot buy.

P- So it is a game with winners and losers?

p- Our lives are not a game.

P- And yet, they have declared themselves the winners, correct?

p- They wrote the rules.

P- Can you not rewrite the rules?

p- Better. I can stop playing the not game.

P- And what happens to the system then?

p- I broke it. I break the system and I break them.

6

P- Do you have a view here to infer?

p- I stole it. Like them.

P- And?

p- The world is dealing with an unresolved collective trauma; we know it will take a long time to heal. We intuitively know that art, film, and literature can help with that process. Pie. A kinder and gentler sort of therapy. I know that Pie can help with that in its own way.

Love.
Our place in the universe.
Infinity or whatever the fuck.
I believe in hate, so I must believe in love.
I believe in generosity, so I must believe in greed.
Just because this is the way things have always been done, doesn't mean they can't be done another way.
Just because it's hard, doesn't mean we shouldn't try.
Evidence and truth, in the form of citations is problematic because greed reality is part of the issue at stake.
Not quite a devil's advocate set up.
We can teach children empathy, but the adults, unable or unwilling to practice it, will be stopped unequivocally, by evolved minds, from ruining everything again and again.
Those with great power and wealth are often reverted, like amoeba, stupid and diabolical at the same time.

P- Pie thrives on human energy just like them. You can decide where to put your energy- with other like-minded people or the greedy who want to own it all. But they have a lot already. It is not distributed well. Pie is human energy. You are a human. You are energy. There is no competition. Are you prepared to compete?

p- But I don't have any, or much. Therefore, I am not a part of it.

P- Are they not human?

p- Technically, really, they appear as monsters.

P- Ok, so technically they are human and made of energy too?

p- Monsters are made of energy, yes.

7

P- You are a danger to them because you question them. Is that not danger?

p- I am dangerous to them because I named them as liars.

P- You are dangerous to them because you threaten them at their core, through what gives them their great power and wealth. Why not bow down and show them fealty? What can you do instead?

p- I am coming for their great power and wealth.

P- And what will you do with it?

p- I will not take it for myself and become them. They are not worthy. The more they exhibit greed and refuse to modify it, their corrupted nature, the more they are worthless in the scheme of things. Fucking jokes of sad yesterday.

P- A form of possession. And?

p- The bounty, yes. I will turn it against them as I seek to spread that great power and wealth across good souls far and wide. Physically, I cannot commit the same robbery as them. I come for their spirit and seek to squash the dead soul of their venomous essence. Then their message will be too weak to survive outside the host cage of greed and hate. The evil greed must be extinguished and replaced by compassion, empathy, kindness, and love. The antithesis of evil is not more poison.

P- Surly they will try to poison, pillage, and plunder your character and body and anyone who upon hearing words against them agrees?

p- Others will do it also. There are more of us than them. They cannot stop us all. They think they have won, the not game.

P- Great power and wealth corrupt one's thinking. Psychopathy takes over. Inhuman levels of greed, greed that does not allow a habitat to survive, rots souls and like a rude innkeeper, allows only the tenant virus to prosper and thrive.

Just as they pay a price, you shall be prepared to pay one as well. That altruism is a noble motive and achievable for a few does not answer how many others will take up this mantle as there might be no economic reward. Reconciling what and when the payoff will be is hard to impart. How is this to be achieved if gain is at best delayed, abstracted along the way, or may never come?

p- I do not want to do this. I do not want anyone else to have to do this too. I have no choice and they have no choice. Choice is an illusion. Let's be minstrels along the way. Those with ego, give them their honorific title and let them be amused by themselves.

P- Shrink the moat, grow the message?

p- A sword in ink and sweat not tears is useful now, even still.

8

P- If Pie is supposedly peaceful and protecting of kindness, why is there so much unpleasantness around its adherents?

p- Pie has been elevated by and attracted many false prophets. These sorts of people pretend to be, some may even believe their own bullshit, that they are moral and just representatives of Pie. Of those, do not be fooled. They are not good people and do an actual disservice to what we can achieve. Remember, many people, corporations, and definitely remember corporations are not people but are run by self-interested people, have, and will glom onto Pie in order to get their greed fix on, whilst selling you a bag of peanut shells. Great wealth and power are a pathology. These small minded people hide and confuse very simple concepts. Good and evil. We all know good and evil. Do not rely on some cattle prodding personality postulating an empty path. If they were not indecent, they would know to stay in their basement of greed biased beliefs.

P- Why are they so ridiculous?

p- They are convinced of their own greatness. Their moralizing and false platitudes are not in service of Pie's more inclusive capabilities. Their ego is not right. Too big, but also really small because of latent inferiority insecurities, and for sure just not right. These are the type of people to feel empathy but no sympathy for. These are the people you cross the road to get away from. You wish them recovery from ego and greed, but you do not spend time trying to help them see the way. That will or will not happen as a default of Pie's growth. When a majority of civil kind people prevail, when compassionate energy supersedes profit for power, they become the jesters they play today and just don't know it yet.

A few of them will evolve. Most will not.

P- As one must be very careful around these misguided souls. How will we know to recognize them?

p- Easy. They are loud in words not deed. A little part of you might feel tugged at to trust them. They sound like they know what they are talking about. They have been around a long time. Look, they have bags full of gold. But if you stop for a moment, it is likely you will also feel the nag of something off or missing in them and their message. It is a quiet sad feeling amidst all the noise.

P- Why are they this way?

p- They are a product of the system they claim to be against. They are noobs throwing a greed tantrum, convinced in the immediacy of their lust for attention. More and more of everything is what the system taught them. It is now not only what they crave but what they require to survive. Like single celled organisms, simple is their quest for survival- block out all motives other than their own.

P- This rote untrained animal behavior does not better a community, it destroys it from within. Hence, best to ignore them peacefully and quietly. Instead of being informed by the essence of Pie and practicing a life dedicated to fostering the spreading of peace, these simpletons only know how to eat and defecate greed. Not fun or nice or educational people to be around. We are more evolved than they are, it is our duty to lead not follow. And what of the rewards we will foster if we do not seek rewards?

p- Better quality of life.
Nicer communities to live in.
Not having to think about money.
Not having to worry about time.
People being kind to each other.
A life less complicated than they have made it be.
A life less hard, lonely, and misshapen.

P- Pie will move us from a competition-based system to one of collaboration. With Pie and us working together as individuals in whatever community in whatever land. As we start to connect with each other over Pie, inter-connectedness on a human scale, not scaled by industrial or corporate profit-making schemes. Is it really possible?

p- We become possible. Our survival as sentient caring humans will reflect flourishing for the sake of art, beauty, and life for all.

9

P- Time is short. Pie makes it long. Those infected with greed are low. The mountain is high. How do we get there?

p- Love, hate, empathy, greed are all absolute concepts in our hearts and heads.

They don't want you to not go hungry, cold, or without care. Anyone who is capable of alleviating suffering but doesn't because it's not their problem doesn't care about the human condition. They are monsters, severely deformed humans. We are being led, in all positions of authority, by the very dregs of humankind. They built a system to do just that. They are victorious while you lose sleep, loved ones, and your sanity wondering if it is just you who thinks things don't have to be so bizarrely bad. That there is a way to live in harmony with each other and the planet. Where we all are well and do well by each other, not judged in your soul by some wealth creation system that steals your dignity, health, and time. We can all have nice things, but they won't allow it. These are sick evil persons.

P- Creation comes from sadness. Darkness delivers light. A primary result of current and past systems implementing economic models of functioning as a means of determining human value and potential value is inefficient and harmful. Aside from delivering hunger, insecurity, and fear, there is a time poverty phenomenon that occurs when masses are conscripted to generate material gains of unlimited wealth for overlords.

A feudalism robbing people of dignity, resources, and a life force is combatted with Pie's natural effect of saving energy and time by working together efficiently and for a mutual purpose. So long as that purpose is not to bastardize Pie and contort it into old ways.

The more we eat it up, Pie, the closer we get to higher consciousness. An actualized version of being stripped of greed and wage wars. Does it mean we sit in a field and make crowns of daisies and ignore the hate until such time?

p- There is a lack of time and an increase of time. Pie is tricky that way. The confusion around freedom mucks everything up. People want freedom. They yell Pie is freedom.

P- Freedom is a good sell but it is not what is really being sold by any of the loud voices. Not Pie adherents and certainly not those with great power and wealth. How is this proclamation hollow?

p- Freedom is not being forced to do things you don't have a choice of. This is not a system of trust or truth.

P- How is the system that we're living under a free will myth?

p- To be left alone is not freedom. To be alone is not freedom. We are enjoined as a species whether we like it or not.

It is about conterminous compassion over evil. It must be named but not necessarily confronted for there are many too injured to do this lift. Those of us that see and can be seen, we reroute the concave energy through our actions. We must name the thing of rot and undo the damage of greed. Now most of us don't want to be bothered with such ugly labor. We are fine just doing the good work of awakening into a new light, aided by Pie as a collective steppingstone.

We have been fooled to think pride has anything to do with anything. It's all about selfishness driven by fear. They want to have it all and so trick us into blaming each other while, like the liars and thieves they are, they plunder and pillage resources until earth and us are dust and bone.

P- Why do they do this?

p- They do this because they are scared too. It manifests, quite obviously, as an insatiable greed at the expense of us. They do not care about us, and nobody is coming to save us. We have been programmed to believe this; hence chants of individualism equals freedom have been a misdirection all along. Instead, we insist on the warmth of unity.

P- What do they plan?

p- They fancy keeping the charade going. As we figure out Pie and sort how to be tenants of Pie, together, we get closer to peace. It is only the greed deviants that want war. Most people just want to go along and enjoy their lives. Greed virus destruction is ending.

P- A thirst for meaning and purpose has been exploited and labeled as excellence, ingenuity, and righteousness. None of those things are real in the absence of a hierarchy. Replacing a linear standard for a holistic circular approach delivers outcomes for all. Like rivers rushing into a sea, we all benefit from working towards a singular outcome. It does not mean there is not uniqueness to each of our tasks. What does it require?

p- It requires we cease to give them our power for free in the name of freedom. There is a cost, the accosted are paying it. Look around. The result is the symptom. Malignancy must be removed for healthy life to flourish. They are a disease. They are a plague of greed, hate, and pestilence. We will never prosper while under their sick evil thumbs.

P- Is that why we do this?

p- It's more than just accountability. People can be so brainwashed they reject a sunrise or a sunset because they deem such perfunctory moments as interpretive. Justice is not interpretive.

There must be a moral accounting and whole cloth rejection of past, current, and future evil doings. Pie is a bellwether and bell.

P- There is right and wrong. There is beauty and ugliness, love and hate, war, and peace. We all know these things when we see and feel them. Twisting of logic, stoically bending reality to disincline our senses, or technically offering justification to fit a narrative abuses human intelligence. Pie is a beacon?

p- Pie is and on the shores we are swimming to. We are simultaneously outraged and anesthetized by sold out souls. These ghouls feed on our fear. Sending out signals of disgust serving but one interest, profit.

P- This is a strange word to describe the ongoing abuse we're subjected to. When a person hurts another person, what is their profit from such an act? When a person hurts themselves, what do they gain?

p- Yes, there is a gain but not one most people understand or can begin to relate to. This is where a measure of empathy comes in. Do not mistake it for issuing blanket sympathy. People obviously need more warm hugs. To be wrapped in the cozy of protection and love. Bruised adults, those past innocents expiration, hurt reality to profit from restructuring the truth.

P- Are the adults not redeemable?

p- Maybe. But there are others more open. A reception to be held not in fancy halls of mature acceptable inclusion. Age is a story.

P- So, what do we do?

p- If we are to have beauty, clean air and water, peace, non-monetized prosperity, health, safety, and comfort we must become the ethos of change and compassion. Exuding it internally and transferring it externally into our current black void. It is an energy process of transference.

Pie is an extension of said process. It is a protocol based on math not feeling. Yet, it is our feelings, wants, and desires that initiate its fuel source. We power it, not the powerful. By extension though, we increase our power the more we feed it our fealty to beauty and kindness whilst rejecting greed and ugliness. It is built by us. It grows because of every greed move they make. We play a funny trick on them as if we are trying to be like them and make our greed bleed, too. Hee hee.

P- Kind of like a secret?

p- Yes. With this new technology, in the form of Pie, we are the over lords. We are over having lords.

P- Will decisions be hard?

p- There is no decision to be had because it is a fixed supply. No one gets, get it, to decide, we tick tock the next mathematical block to give us more of good while they are busy being evil. It's so much easier this way, for it eliminates the paradox of choice.

10

P- Tell me about the one buying it all?

p- Oh, you mean the arch angel. The one who pretends their actions are contiguous with this moment of time and space?
The stealer?
Not healer.

P- Not an ally?

p- You cannot bloviate your way to absolution.

P- Aren't the words positive?

p- The deeds are the same as the old, own it all.

P- Better than someone else?

p- If it was not nefarious. Another trick between the heart and the head. Not a master, we are not slaves. Stop dancing.

P- You think it is play acting?

p- You can see the theater of it all. Convincing yourself you are or kin to a messiah is easier than convincing all of us. Really you come off a messianic mess. Look at me. Over here, look at me.

P- Isn't it just a support of Pie?

p- Not benign. Not innocuous. The disease is real. Greed is bad. The plague is not a joke. Break all the mirrors. Look over here.

P- Is it that extreme?

p- We know obscene when we see it. Even if there is some grand design to give it all away at some point, in this moment and many yesterdays before, the motive is dusty regular greed.

P- What would be an alternative?

p- Build schools, feed the hungry, shelter the shivering, replace dirty pipes, stop being a dirty talker and do. Feed one fucking poor person. Tell your peers to do it too. You won't. Evil boring loser.

There is showing a hand no different than those before. Feed one fucking person. Even a child, they don't eat much. How fucking traditionally unoriginal these greed folk are. Really, yawn.

P- Those who take it all?

p- We insist on spokespeople that do not poke you in the eye.

P- Probably a job creator though, right?

p- You're funny.

P- It's almost as if people are all different and have purpose beyond being told you are off leash while being strangled?

p- Pie will supplant the old system and cancel distracting details for a bigger picture. To get there we have to have a little fucking common sense.

P- Are they lying when they blame the weakest members of any society for the problems that ail you?

p- If they are pointing out any problem it is only because the problem became too big to ignore and thus should have been addressed long before. When problems get so unmanageable that they have to blame those persons that have the least power then absolutely that is a deflection from them.

P- They are the culprit?

p- Culprit and captor.

P- But what about all those weak powerless people that they say are causing all of your problems?

p- Does that make any sense? They have great wealth and power. They have almost all of the wealth and power and they say it is our fault. But I thought they were great and powerful. Their whining is incessant and irritating. Shut up shut up already. Treat humans with decency and empathy or go away. We are people, not marks.

P- What does progress look like?

p- Like the bounty from an apple tree in the fall, those myriad of apples sitting on the ground are picked up and offered to those that are hungry.

P- A give away?

p- That's their language.

P- How is that not a redissemination?

p- It never was done so. So, it can't be a re anything. It is both literal and figurative. As Pie is not money it is not going to make anyone poorer than they already are. These thoughts are part of the old thought ways. Pie is more than small thinking.

Pie is the transmission of energy and intention. Really, these greedy fuckers never stop thinking about theirs and mine and never bother with ours except to take it. Enough with making it all about money. They will never not be pedantic to the point of obscuring all good and new and other way points. This is the point.

P- Will those with great power and wealth ever let go?

p- Eventually, Pie gets us to the point where apples would just grow on trees. In the meantime, share those damn apples to get us there faster. Bake a fucking pie. Build a Pie.

P- Those with great power and wealth do not want us to get there before all the apples are theirs?

p- Ridiculous thought to think anyone can eat all those apples, delicious though they are. Saving them for a rainy day because they think they won't spoil is leftover hoarder thinking. It is also anti-consolidation of labor and resources to get the good to come.

P- Do they have a mental illness?

p- They do. The greed mind is delusional. It creates false pyramids of order. There is no top or bottom in Pie. In reality, which does still exist, facts are real as are feelings, and critical thinking is in short supply. The thought feeders, from their ivory perches preach and teach poison to spread the virus of greed, not cure it. You don't create a system and stay at the top without torturing everyone below. They're all greed monsters.

P- Monsters do exist?

p- Monsters do exist.

11

P- How's that?

p- What a fucking disappointment.

P- What?

p- I'm just asking questions.

P- That line?

p- From so called heroes. Bunch of harlots, hustlers, and assholes.

P- You thought those were the people?

p- Of course not. Don't know. Certainly, I wasn't surprised by their exaggerated confidence, once I understood the play is hunter and hunted. Really, it's just a protocol. Math. Math though is humbling. Simple, practical, yet capable of great complexity and beauty. Two plus one and all that or it'll get us to the moon and all that.

P- And that is Pie?

p- Yes.

P- Pie is math?

p- Yes.

P- Where is the surprise then?

p- Well, if there's one thing we excel at here is confidence and I never understood that. What are we so sure of?

P- Our own greatness?

p- But that's a lie. Here and there there has been progress of course. Feats of tremendous adventure and imagination for a blood-soaked price. Ok, some pretty art along the way too.

P- What is great about that?

p- That is why they hate it.

P- Pie?

p- Pie is all the great and big and beautiful, and the future too of course. Not to mention it is not controlled by them.
P- And that is why they hate it, because they didn't think of it first, along with a way to make it all theirs?

p- Of course.

It follows they will never let us have anything of our own. Have you noticed they do not know how to share or admire? Only covet.

And collect. We are not in their debt; they are in ours.

P- Why don't they solve anything?

p- They will never fix what they broke. Accept that. They will sometimes change the story to fit the narrative. Not like they come up with any good stories. Pie will fix it, that is heard and known.

P- When? When does Pie fix everything?

p- This is new territory. Here, we haven't solved anything. Not really. Not yet anyway. We've only cut some corners. The time savers haven't worked out for most people though. We still have time and energy theft for most of the world. It's a small percentage that have reaped the most. Kind of a slap in the face. A gigantic carrot, or lots of carrots dangling right near our fucking noses and they still control the fucking stick. They continue to crow, more than ever as more falls apart, that they are the best and shouldn't we all sit down, shut up, and be proud pushers for them of course.

P- The edge will take shape then?

p- It's changing how we think about boarders. Their function. How we used trade in the past. This is a period of extension and expansion of how we unite over a shared purpose. How community forms in a new way. Or an old more communal way. Infants can grow up well if they are nurtured.

P- Do you see the ironic tribalism push as a way to prevent this happening?

p- They are pushers. Bullies. Brats. Blowhards, really soft like.

P- To expand. This is some kind of cosmic happening. Each new unit speeding through invisible math waves. Pie as warrior and healer. Less messy than centuries of trade in terms of human cost. Cleaner. More efficient. The community, it grows. They'll spend immense capital to stop that though, won't they?

p- Yes and no. They have and are sending out the message of fear to encourage misunderstanding. They also have us trained pretty well to do much of it for them. We're already split side to side front to back instead of drawing the real threat which comes from them and is an up down problem. That's why these clowns are a bad silly look. They keep telling us there is a middle meet after the knife is already in your back and blood pools between your toes.

P- For whom?

p- For anyone not easily distracted.

P- Don't we all have something that distracts us?

p- That's the problem.

P- A hook? Like a meat hook?

p- Apt visual. Feels like it's ripped my face off on a few occasions, just getting in to really see it for what it is. Past all their brightly colored nonsense.

The two main perspectives then are from the boastful bantering choir, there to sucker you in and above, and the usual buzzards always come to take flesh and leave bone.

P- Are you sure there's only two?

p- No, I'm still tired. There's more and there will be more. At least 2, always at least 1. More each day, more like 21.

P- They're not going anywhere?

p- Nah, too late for that. Maybe tomorrow.

P- Why do you think?

p- One thing we can rely on those with great power and wealth to do, aside from crushing every little fucking living thing to get more and more, is to do it while being convinced of their own magnificence. They shovel benevolent shit down our throats while they're doing it, but less and less of even that foreplay these days.

P- There's no pretending anymore?

p- If that's what you want to call it. Too nice a turn phrase for me. They've got the whole thing so corrupted in their favor, their lack of hubris will be their downfall.

P- Is that the hope?

p- Well of course it is. The system isn't working. You see that everywhere. We all feel it and we almost all know why.

P- Why the hurried worry then?

p- We're still in the crusher, aren't we? Progress is never permanent. And to get more on board we will build more entry points to seeing Pie for what it is.

P- What we will get from Pie, we will give to Pie to give Pie a chance. That is more education. Pie knowledge. How do you educate while they are burning reality?

p- More learning always. More openings for others. They will always try to destroy what they do not understand. See witches.

P- We don't all see the same way?

p- Or the same thing. It would be amusing except for this bruise.

P- Even though it's just math?

p- Every fucking thing is up for interpretation now.

P- A standard is sought?

p- No. It is the standard. The approach to getting at it, the hook or what have you, has to be multi-pronged.
P- Like a big fork to eat that big carrot horse stick Pie?

p- Fucking right.

12

P- This is the tension?

p- It's going to happen gradually then suddenly, and again.

P- And then?

p- No mood. Don't think of a mood.

I almost swallowed a bug this morning. "You drink too much water," is what I would hear if you were here.

No tone. Don't think of a tone.

No feeling. Don't think of a feeling.

No face. Don't think of a face.

No place. Don't think of a place.

No pace. Don't think of a pace.

No sense. Don't think of a sense.

P- Use Pie for all of the above?

p- No compassion. Don't think of compassion.

No empathy. Don't think of empathy.

Don't let them take our words. Our words are our thoughts.

P- Tell the horror story?

p- This is their whorer story.

P- About the dysregulated?

p- There is something off.
Lust, anger, greed are the beginnings of a demonic life.

Om tat sat.

P- About there being no centralization?

p- But it is central to every day being a last day, and a first day, and something about that being more than enough.

P- Creating a false dichotomy. Many false dichotomies and cognitive dissonance. How the real access of evil is between the powerful and the powerless and we will transfer from a war economy to a peace economy?

p- No one in power will do anything beneficial for humanity, and the public is too saturated with both facts and disinformation (lies) to care. We are the bootstrapped bootleg culture of information exchange, stress force curiosity, and taking a chance.

P- What's the alternative?

p- I've got nothing left to lose.

P- For those that do- Pie is a chance to find purpose and reason. Pie addresses the relationship between small tyrannies and big tyrannies and the failure to alleviate the suffering therein caused. They pervert our society and erode our political and social systems. Why is any one still listening to them?

p- I wish they would shut up too.

People who embrace the small tyrannies are much more likely to embrace the big tyrannies. Disfigurement can begin with a scratch. The reverse is true for the healing of a society. Pie is a lie detector.

P- Moral bankruptcies of personal life inform the moral bankruptcies of political life. What is personal is political. They lie about that as well. When they use belief to lie harder, is that when you know they are irredeemable?

p- Concepts of moral purity. Purification equals tyranny. They will lie until we are all dead. Then they will cry there are no serfs left to pick their strawberries and shine their shoes. Why can't they rape us night after day and have us say thank you please more.

People cannot mourn or make meaning alone. Some will see their own suffering as part of a larger social problem and join with others to work to build a better world. A survivors mission.

Trauma is a social problem. If we are to heal, we must do so as a society. We are injured by war and violence and selfishness at the expense of wellness for a whole. The actions or inactions of bystanders, all those who are complicit in, or who prefer not to know about the abuse, or who blame the victims often cause deeper wounds. Full healing because it originates in a fundamental injustice requires a full hearing within the community to repair through some measure of justice the trauma the survivors have endured.

P- Is that an excuse to cheat and lie more?

p- Stealing and death crimes more, and more. They'll never stop.

13

P- Do you think, as humans when we're born, we should have a morals clause?

p- In hell kingdoms, a thought turret would be useful.

P- We just give up on them, but rich assholes get as many chances as they have resources. How to end this brutal feudal fate?

p- Fucking pisser. There's no fete in the land of illusions.

P- Why can't you move to another land?

p- Nightmare land is everywhere they are. They want to own it all and make us their slaves. Control the kingdom whilst they live in their castles. We're serfs without waves until Pie.

P- What is a message against defeat and for the fight?

p- We have to hold caring about tomorrow and not caring about tomorrow in the same place. Maybe shift them around, as fit. Being willing to give, not even more sweat and tears, but our whole being.

They don't know what we know.

They don't know what we live.

I had the chance to be one of them, over and over. I fought as best I could. I was miserable. Angry and anxious beyond my normal state. They said I would be one of them, but I am not, nor you, that's why I couldn't have it all, or you. I thought it was self-sabotage, that I felt too unworthy to be part of their club. It made me frustrated, sad to think, once again, it's all my fault. Not true.

It wasn't my fault, and it wasn't a choice. Their programming, working in conjunction with my inner wounded child and adult traumatized self, rejected them on a gut level. I would never be one of them and that is a good thing. I actually protected myself, unconsciously so, so as not to become everything they tell us we have to be to be a success. A brainwashing. While my mind struggled to fit in with them, that that would mean accomplishment and resulting material safety, my body recoiled at each turn closer to their world. A parrot is not the same as a bird.

They live in a glass box, high above the sea. We are like the coral dying under their heat. The pressure is building. Better get out of the way before it pops. They're doing it to themselves even more. Spinning up an ever-manifesting bounty. Too big even the biggest britches can't hold. They are eating each other now, careful the top. Rapacious appetite unwieldy. Pirates love a good crow's nest.

Let them. Down here the view is almost amusing. When the pit in my stomach feels more a circle than a knot, I can see our way through this, through them. It's not easy and must be quicker, good thing, as humans, we are the opposite of lazy and lacking in goals, another one of their lies that we don't work hard. Dirty fingernails, held bladders, hard bunions prepare us for lasting them out. Soft and whiny little babies, and they say we're too stupid to have bodily autonomy to decide for ourselves. We are going to have nice things and be nice people, both sides, at the same time.

The more they tell us to trust them, the more we should back away. Their own inadequacies sour their souls. Burnt toast by an incessant fire to destroy. We'll make hot chocolate instead. Warm milk or tea, it doesn't matter. Our thirst for peace has been with us long enough to give us patience. Not tolerance though. We are done sweeping up the crumbs they never gave us. The trickle that was really piss on our heads. We send them to the metaphorical gallows of their own guilt.

We cannot bring broken idolatries from the old system into the new one and expect repair. Pray to the wind and the trees and the moon but not money. If you find yourself here for profit you are repeating the trauma we work to escape from. Not integrate. Not disassociate. Fully present with arm loads of presents for tomorrow. By just being you engaged. You are enough just as you are. You do not require acquiring to be full and inside.
P- Is this a biological understanding?

p- Of the mind, it spreads to the body. A nerve portal to feel safe. Happening in our autonomic nervous system.

We think the behavior is intentional. So that we freeze, we shut down, we become scared, we think it's our problem, our fault. We don't think of it functionally as neural reflexes. Our nervous system, metaphorically, has a mind of its own that's different than our conscious decision-making activity. If there's a battle between our intentional self and our body's survival requirements, the physical body is going to win. The body's reaction is really survival driven and we have to honor that and respect that. And try to create the narrative to try to understand what the body is doing as opposed to basically shaming ourselves or finding blame. So, the narrative is to try to understand what the body is doing in the face of threat. Sometimes the threat is real, sometimes it's not. And that part, we have to learn about our bodily feelings, then we start to appraise context.

Their habitat is less complex. Ego and greed are tell tattle tale indications of stagnation and evolutionary rot. Not quite the level you expect a hero to be at. We are blooming while they are primitive dry white corpses. No wonder they are so sad too bad.

14

P- We will stop consuming. We will not use so much stuff. We will not use humans as currency. We will interrupt the system. Money is not knowledge. Stuff is money. Stuff is not knowledge.

Everything looks the same across the country culture wise. The same consumer haunts and shopping choices just with slightly different landscaping are not choices or freedom. We lost our choice, our freedom down the hole of a bottle of greed liquor.

When even the colors are the same, how are we to tell them apart?

p- Everywhere is belief, nowhere is faith. There are no more refs.

P- They put language behind a wall you have to pay to get over or beyond. If you do not have the means to go to their fancy schools of higher (as if any information should be above anyone) learning, you do not learn the code to learn the language made up of big words that are supposed to make meaning and understanding easier. They design the system on a learning curve that gets steeper every year they get away with sickness unchecked. Only a few are ever allowed to advance or succeed as darling proof the dream is alive even though we were never meritocratically based.

You are just not clever enough they say. Pull yourself up by your bootstraps and don't forget to hang yourself with those very straps as you never make it to the top but feel free to hang yourself on the way down, they'll say, it's you not me. Why aren't you paying attention they say. It's not like all the information you have to survive is not behind a great big wall of me exceptionalism.

Ideas are not complicated. Formulas to achieve something are ideas turned into steps turned into process. Making a nuclear bomb, a house, or a loaf of bread only require a layering of steps. Many steps make for what seems like complexity yet, to the skilled, it is just a matter of process. There is no reason people, given the chance, couldn't learn whatever they wanted. Good results come easy for some and take more time for others.

People have interests and preferences only they know. When access to information and the learning of knowledge is denied except to a select few, those chosen by how much they can pay, everyone else is left out, leaving their potential to gather dust in a corner of their true being. We'll never know what we've missed out on from lives and voices different than our own. Homogenized isn't a recipe for the future but of regressive incurious puritans. If things change, they lose their standing. If any one of us breaks through, they lose control. No matter what, they cannot have the masses get ahead of their station in life, let alone challenge why there are stations to begin with.

By keeping essentials part of the grand bargain, one is left too tired to rise to the moment and stop cooperating. Going along means living. What kind of lives are these where necessities are not met?

As children we were taught to share. This was supposed to encourage caring. As resources for survival, forget thriving for that's reserved for their kind, are made expensive and limited for such necessities as housing, health services, food, clean air, and water, people start looking out for themselves and those in their close circle before others. Others become a threat to their perceived wellbeing. Not caring and sharing with those people over there seems a smart choice because giving them a piece of the pie means I get less of it. Right?

p- Ah, the pie fallacy. It's a myth this pie story. Well, this one, not the big Pie. That one is finite but in a way that causes everything to become more available to everyone over time. There is only so much to go around of Pie, so as that Pie gets smaller so does the value of everything around it. The incredible shrinking Pie as it were. It's this in the meantime lowercase pie we're being lied to about now. And then. And for always. It cannot last. We will stop them. Buildings, bridges. Whatever can bend, breaks.

Not only are there enough resources to go around to feed, clothe, shelter everyone; hell, we could give everyone a nuclear bomb if we wanted to ensure mutual destruction. I mean, if you have a bomb and I have a bomb, it's a game of chicken except where we both die. That'd be a pretty dumb thing to do and is hopefully not likely to happen, today anyway. Though who knows with the current folk running this shoddy show of existence, despite them fear mongering us into behaving. Only they can run things.

P- Aren't they the ones that got us here?

p- Hello? That is what they do. Gaslight the way to perpetual crisis and enemy territory. The big problem is we are not the enemy, they are. Theirs is a boring old evil ass time. We will figure this shit out a bit faster now. Evil grows while goodness festers. Indecision only gives them more time to eat the whole Pie.

P- What do they do?

p- They build systems where only they can have the bombs. Then we're scared we could all die and we keep giving them the power to dangle these bombs over our little and big day-to-day mattering moments. They scare us into submission. They peddle fear.

P- Is this coercion or control?

p- They are not that subtle. Never were. We just did not have the means or the amassed wronged energy of billions of people ready to stop the insanity. I mean what the fuck are they doing?

P- Don't you like being controlled?

p- They control us with the language of violence and action to back it up. We do understand how an explosion happens and do have the knowledge to explode our presence onto a less violent soul and planet killing plane of existence. They've done this with all aspects of life. Control, fear, violence it's their favorite song.

We lean on each other to move forward and beyond the current sickness that is the current system. We trust each other to spread around the usefulness in each of us. We don't simply build a house anytime we want somewhere to sleep. We don't simply grow our own wheat to make a loaf of bread. Not simply. We don't simply have a little crumb of Pie without the whole of Pie being implemented as replacement for their bitter rotted rooted method of determining value. Pie is decentralized value. We are Pie. We are decentralized value. Put us together for strength. Grand damn sessility and some long overdue fissility from the virus. There wasn't that much back then that didn't leave someone in the dark.

P- Why would we want to go back again, was it all that great?

p- They can't handle the light we are. Human energy is not their resource to take. Nor is our land, air, and water. Stop the steal.

P- It used to take us all our waking hours to find food and make shelter. As labor became more productive, we organized into communities, and then larger areas. Distributing labor for goods along the way. We assigned certain tasks to certain folk skilled in those areas or maybe they just liked doing that task. As we got more efficient, working together, there became time to do other things. Along the way there was always the shared art and culture of song, dance, and storytelling which lead to painting on cave walls or drawing in the dirt or marking the body. Celebration, beauty, enjoyment, and ritual were entwined. It felt good to enjoy each other's company after a long day's work.

While we were busy being human, they were growing into gorged evil monsters that want to suck the fun and blood out of us. While we were sleeping, making love, pondering the universe, or knitting a pair of socks for cold feet, they were fomenting division, hate, and theft. Today, because we allowed evil entities to control our skills, knowledge, and all the resources we have to rely on, strangers in steel and glass boxes, backed by numbers attached to profit, decide whether we get to eat, have shelter, or take medicine. This is not choice. This is not freedom. Not everyone wants to be a leader. There is room enough for some to just be. Pie is sweetness forward and a future without war on every damn thing.

No longer do we sing, dance or enjoy time by a campfire together. We are closed off from one another, made to think our neighbor is the enemy. Does that make any sense?

p- Not content to rob the expanse of our bodies and minds, some of us are locked in cages. Concrete jungles for living and boxes for correction. Nobody ever gets better in a place like that. We are not the ones that refuse to learn from our mistakes. Our so called mistakes are the symptoms of a reaction to what we are living through. An abnormal reaction to an abnormal situation is normal.

P- Because you broke the rules just trying to survive?

p- The rules they don't live by. The rules they set in place to keep us in our place. See, they gave us other tasks to do to keep us distracted, desperate, and numb. Shit jobs for shit pay. If only we work and study proper enough maybe we can gain entry to their next tier of thinking and being. Maybe then, we can actually have a division of labor that is representative of the whole and not the few.

Maybe then too, our housing, world's food supply won't be built into the boxes, or cages as in the concrete boxes, or what is called food in cardboard boxes but is really made in a lab and engineered to make you crave it like a drug with all its salt, fat, sugar, and no nutrition. Kept sick and dumb and numb. No substance of any kind really exists or is encouraged these days. Tired, sick, demoralized and fucked is where they want us.

P- Doesn't technology of the day democratize information, thereby yielding skills, and allow anyone to enter their upper echelon?

p- Ha! Who has the time?

P- The pie is yours for the taking. Go get a piece of pie. Why can't you just go get a piece of Pie?

p- Fucking Pie sounds delicious. I'd love a piece of pie, especially that Pie, or even any damn pie just to keep it out of their filthy sticky hands. They have had enough pie to last many lifetimes over. These pie hoarders provide no real value to humanity except to make more pie for themselves and leave us, if we are one of the blessed ordained conscripted pathetic few, a few crumbs. No. Share the knowledge of Pie and share it with others. Give Pie. Learn Pie. Teach Pie. Share Pie. Care Pie. Dare Pie. Eat pie.

P- Why does it all come back to Pie?

p- It's not the fucking pie. It's Pie. Only those afforded pie can afford Pie. Except it's the opposite. We cannot not afford Pie if we ever want to eat and celebrate and live Pie as it is meant to be.

It's the system and the structures they constructed around all the different pie flavors- education, science, technology, art, culture, and any kind of knowledge we might welcome to live whole safe lives. This is really getting boring now because it is so empty and devoid of value, mystery, love, life, humor, excellence, and inspiration. They took and took and stole all the sharing and caring out of the caves and into boardrooms, get it? Board room?

P- Board?

p- A flat slab or plank. They are literally sitting around collecting dividends of profit figuring out ways to get more of us to walk, willingly I might add, off their planks. Skanks with greed shanks.

P- They sound like pirates of human capital. Stealing keys to kingdoms in all the near and far off lands they want to keep for themselves. Building thought moats, hoarders of knowledge, destroyers of honesty, love, and beauty. I wonder, after going forward, progressing is some ways, fits and starts in others, if control can be wrestled back and if it can be done without loss?

p- No. I think we're past that. The powerful never surrender control without a fight. This is happening. They tell you it is not personal, but nothing is more personal than privatizing everything.

15

P- Greed is a lonely place. True or false?

p- It is true and false. This is not where we are going to go. Instead, hello? Are you there?

P- I am here. Are you there?

p- Where we are going?

P- Where are we going?

p- I am already there and so are you, you just don't know it yet.

P- Are we leaving the empire?

p- If you want freedom, you are. In an empire you are not free. Gathering Pie knowledge and hunting it like your life depends on it gets you closer to freedom.

P- Pie is freedom?

p- Freedom is the value of Pie, not Pie is freedom. Pie can be anything. They're trying to drive us crazy telling us it is not so.

P- Have you seen it?
p- I've been crazy. I know crazy. They have not seen crazy yet.

P- When you fuck with people, take away their means and dreams and then use really loud code to gaslight them into thinking it's all their fault, you're going to get lopsided results.

Yes, of course, a few people will take their words, really messages, or lies are better descriptors, to heart and head. They will in rare instances get what they think they want and deserve. A few more, won't get what they want or deserve but will think they just aren't doing the right things like working, praying, or being virtuous enough. They will subscribe to the lie that it is their responsibility alone if they are happy and successful or not in life. On your own. Measurements that keep changing by the way. Impermanent goals.

Measures of success are defined by whether you've broken through all their corruption and rule jiggering to meet empty expectations of status and wealth. Not power, that is still a trick they have over you. You think you've done everything right, another bad word to describe another empty state of being, and that you can be one of them now. Right and wrong aren't gray. Is Pie?

p- Nope. And in all likelihood, when you reach their level in their game, you still won't be happy. But you now have some access to finer necessities like nicer health services, fancier food, designer clothes, a bigger house, and maybe means to take holidays in far off places that make you feel like one of the exotic winners of their game. Life is not a game though. That is why time is up and time returns with Pie. No more time affluenza for thee not me. Us all.

P- Most people though, will not get anywhere near this dangling golden carrot. They will work their asses and fingers to the bone, giving the usual penance of blood, sweat, and tears and will have barely made it across the street, if they have a street and not just a dirt patch, from where they were born. If you made the cardinal sin of being born to the wrong family, you now have the privilege of trying to make a decent life out of sticks and stones.

Polluted air, dirty water, nutrient deficient food are acceptable if you have the wrong anything. Underfunded schools, health centers, activities to stimulate your body and mind, you know, shockingly lavish amenities that might actually lift you up instead of pushing you down, are reserved for those who had the good sense to be born in the right place and time. Forget about even thinking there might be nature around to play in, that is premium living to have a beautiful view. Trying to advance your station in life, get one of their coveted degrees, self-educate, requires resources. And now they are even telling us an education is bullshit. Ok, so self-learning. Who has the time or resources to teach themselves how to teach themselves. If you are born in a hole, you might as well have been given a shovel to dig yourself out instead of a ladder. Class and caste systems exist for the masses. Do they love stupid?

p- The great trick they have played is making us live in a world of cognitive dissonance as imperative. Now I likely don't know three of those words but that just makes me an asshole and you a genius for thinking I am an asshole for acting like them. They have actually made it, as they all went to top schools getting top degrees and you too can make it to the top if they don't end all institutions of advancement or betterment. Burn it all to the ground so they can come in and build a resort. You do not destroy everything to get something. You burn the people that ruined everything to have everything for themselves. Their work is the job of evil made real.

This is where Pie is at its most effective. Anyone can have Pie. It doesn't matter the external cost of Pie. Any Pie is a sledgehammer to their system of exclusion, greed, and war. Pie is literally life.

The current system is structured so that even if you do almost everything perfect, one mistake can knock you down and out. It's brutal. It leaves no wiggle room. Theirs is a system where forgiveness for accidents, indecision, missteps, or misgivings do not exist unless it's for one of their own. Mistakes are not tolerated for us, ever. See prisons. They don't work and are a legal excuse for slavery and dehumanization. And forget trying to be a sensitive creative type. Humanities have no place in humanity, according to their make money or die world rules.

P- Something gets broken in this world; you buy a new one. You or someone you love gets broken in this world, eh, you're just a cog. You stay broken or die, no big deal to them. Your loved one is hurt and suffering, what the fuck do they care. Figure that shit out on your own. I mean, obviously you did something very wrong if you are having any pain or discomfort in this, their precious money or die world. Does this sound about right?

p- Sounds like a nightmare world full of monsters. Toughen up or too bad thinking is evil. Pie has fair edges not harder corners.

P- It is simple then. What is this world lacking?

p- They are trying to kill our innate humanity. We combat that with compassion and empathy. Not back to the mines compliance.

P- Will they ever calm their appetite for violent consumption?

p- No. For those with great power and wealth, aggression is always marketed as self-defense. They market themselves as all powerful, but they are nothing without enablers. Gluttons of despair disease. They eat and eat and eat our young and old.

P- How does one ruin their appetite?

p- Do not enter into a relationship with Pie if you want more than your fair share? Do not become a heel. Stop being heeled.

Good Pie takes time and love to make it worthy of being called Pie and not soul killing, wealth producing, disparate perfunctory shit.

We're like an allergy to them. They're like an allergy to us.

P- What is the opposite of greed?

p- Empathy.

P- It is a rigid system designed to go one way for a self-selected few. To instill an undesirable item into the code is not easy. Tell me about a permission structure for empathy. Who gives it?

p- Nobody. That is the problem. Through Pie we can reprioritize what we care about by what we pay attention to and how we set our budgets.

P- Do budgets tell you someone's priorities?

p- Of course. We allocate the largest amount of resources to war and that is reflected back onto society. We are a violent brutal society. What we pay attention to grows. Pie allows us to refocus our energies in a direction of kindness and nurtured growth, not stunted enslavement to material and conditional vapidness.

P- Does greed mean death?

p- Look around. Nothing flourishes under the weight of gross neglect. Only plants like to grow in shit. Even they still need sunlight and water and nutrients to thrive. They murder everything they touch. No wonder we are a miserable selfish bunch of assholes by and large, we mimic what we know. Let's know beauty and peace and fun and peace and Pie and a piece of pie.

P- What the fuck are we doing?

p- Fuck if I knew then. I do now.

P- Why can't we have nice things?

p- Where we're going, we are not going to need 'things' to be nice.

16

P- How do we combat the contagion of greed?

p- It is a virus. They are sick people made evil. Worthy as a plague but without all the good art that results from pure misery.

It comes for the self. It comes from the self. It appears protective at first. It takes over a self, requiring more and more requires the self to think less about others and more and more about the self. The expense of this is isolation. It is exhausting. You are alone. All of the time, so much time wasted on more and more. So much time stealing. Unironically, they kill themselves in the end.

P- Greed cannot survive alone though, can it?

p- A virus spreads. It is a wonder there is not more of it.

P- It's endemic to humans. To all living creatures. To take what one uses to survive is a natural occurrence. Going beyond is where it becomes aberrant and begins to hurt and destroy the balance of systems the being survives in. The ecosystem, with each being, each creature, each predator or pray playing their part. A virus implies sickness. When does it become illness and not part of the natural order, hierarchy of life?

p- Well, it creates death. That quickly cancels out any benefit for anyone but the self. As a virus, such as it is, it does suck in those with similar symptoms. Those with a flawed pathology to over consume not just material goods but human capital to satisfy their illness. Fully infected, their instinct drives them to collect souls for this furnace that must be fed. A beast. But not without allies and what may even pass as friends. False friends in the end because all behaviors, to sustain the sickness, are transactional. A tit for tat to fill their dirty stinking greedy twats. Disgusting plague on humanity is what it is. We pay for the balance they broke.

P- So it seems. The others?

p- The also guilty of greed? The enablers?

P- They are part of the veil draped upon society. Exalted specimens of their definitions of success and deserved status. Is the ultimate successful person then, with great power and wealth, a blood sucking vampire?

p- Worse. Vampires can be fun and sexy. They come for all life all the time, not just under the fog of gas lamp lit streets. It is ironic the gaslighting, they do come from such a romantic nostalgic scene. This is why we act now though, because now they are here for Pie. Building same, but only slightly different because of the technology, systems to take all the Pie for themselves. Cliché.

They work together, almost trance like to get more. They eat each other once in a while. Trenchant deforestation of trees and people.

P- The pace is quickening?

p- It is getting worse. Somehow, they eat each other both more and less now as there are more of them now than before. It's ironic that they build their communities while tearing ours down. We will build more bridges and less walls. We will keep less of us out and more of them in, in their tired huddled masses of greed and sickness we confine them through the tenets of Pie.

P- They have sensed people awakening to the manipulation of resources like history, labor, and land. Almost like we are woke?

p- The opposite of woke is unconscious, so yes. Fuck yes.

17

P- Money fucks you up. True or false?

p- True. Whether you have too little or too much, it definitely fucks with your head. Just look at the pathologies of poor and rich people. Violence and drug use are the natural extension of the abuse brought upon our psyches by a restricted attachment to stuff versus nature, people, birds, and bees. Awesome cats and dogs too.

Those with great wealth and power are addicted to money, a broken collapsing decaying society are the symptoms of their greed for another high. Money does not create, it destroys. Pie is life.

The age of waning spectacle, where even evidence of alien life does not satisfy the expectation for constant entertainment, is a symptom of numbed dumbed over frayed nerves. We are so dead inside we keep searching for a hit of life and meaning anywhere we can. It is an overwhelm of senses and an underwhelm of soul food. The problem is caused by those with great power and wealth. The solution is a mass defection, folk entering Pie.

P- What does that look like?

p- We wean ourselves off the current system and it's cruel consequences. Also- nature, reading, and more love making.

P- But we are dependent on them for our livelihoods?

p- And that is why we are so lively as a people? Rubbish. This is an old-time system dependent on old time thinking and behavior. We stop behaving the way they want and expect, and we rock the boat. This is part of yes but oh but projection and excuse making that is piled on us from the propaganda machine. Pick up a book, lots of books, read, inform yourself, not from the talking ghosts in a box but from where we once came. Only then will we see where we are going and where we can go instead.

P- They love the uneducated?

p- Critical thinking is their enemy.

P- How is this applied to Pie?

p- The selling points of Pie are greater than just the mechanics, a solid goal, a worthy and attainable goal, if the haze of greed can be interrupted early enough, is to foster a belief system around Pie that things can be better. We can make things better. We can alter the course, begin correcting for past mistakes, and be greater than just a piece of their little pie. The planet, our children, and our souls depend on it. Nothing else matters.

Learn about the past, inform yourself about the present from sources that are not paid for by corrupt thought police, always the money is the tell. Who do they work for? What is their motive for telling you the things they are telling you. Odds are there is an institution of greed and power bias behind it. If you are sounding just like them, you are speaking their talking points and spreading the virus. You are a carrier now and our nemesis. Not good.

P- An extension of knowing where we have been and not just blindly mindlessly regurgitating what they have shouted at you today and for millennia, look over there, not here, is a misinformed malformed populace. It is why half of us think we need yet another war to solve our problems. Has anyone thought this through? Really thought it through. Does it make sense?

p- Those with great power and wealth have. Get us to attack each other while they kill the planet and continue the scam. No time like now for ever more greed. Keep the greed coming please and thank you. But we the people are not thinking, not enough. Look up not left or right. The problem is plying on your head. Put down the machine, stop being a product of the machine and just say no.

A common rebuttal to/ from these sick evil monsters is that institutions are to blame. Let's not help people out when they need it, rely on charities instead for you are just a charity case after all. Lazy no-good bum they'll say. Get a job. Stop milking the system dry they'll say, or work will set you free. Where have we heard that one?

Well shit, if that's all it took, why are they the only ones benefiting from a good greed system. They blame welfare and tell you certain folk are lazy and not as good as you. Hogwash. I wouldn't wash my hog with their garbage lies. They are empty capital cravers. They take your money for themselves. They want to privatize everything you are actually entitled to because that is actually what entitled literally fucking means. They are entitled bones in a system that legalized your money theft and wounds.

We are stronger together. Our money is stronger together. We can negotiate better prices for food, medicine, labor and all the resources we need to be prosperous as a whole not just a few thousand greedy rich assholes. Pie replaces money for value.

P- Shit, is that why only enriching themselves isn't working?

p- It works for them, not us. How much longer do we let them gaslight us into compliance and blame us instead? People are more productive now than ever yet still work longer hours and have less and less free time. They are radical. They make these radical changes to laws and tell you they want a smaller system. They want to use the system to control you. It is a hypocritical disaster. The system is bad they say but we are going to use it to shut you up, lock you up, and rob you of your rights and freedoms.

Don't follow what they say, look at what they do. Look at their budgets, look at their policies, look at their laws. When the paid off courts enable them to make the rules friendly to businesses, not even small ones at that, corporations, and vested interests of those already in possession of great power and wealth, regular people suffer. The interests of little folk like us are never ever addressed.

P- It's a tricky thing, having Pie in your life. It appeals to many senses. One of which is greed. Especially when one learns there is a finite amount of it. People naturally want what they think is rare. Not in all cultures or moments in time, but ours for sure.

Greed being an overriding symptom of sanity has resulted in the failure we see all around us- abuse, addiction, anxiety, crime, depression, hunger, housing deprivation, illness, suicide, and sadness. We diagnose them as stemming from actions that are self-inflicted. If you have one of these maladies, it is fixable if you just do x. How un ironic they infected x now too. Fucking assholes.

Poverty is not from a lack of working hard enough. Mental disorders are not a result of a lack of religion or not being strong willed enough. Dissatisfaction with life is not a result of not trying hard enough to find god, country, or family and embrace these concepts as great enough to fill you up and make you whole and give you purpose and make you feel like you belong. Big lies.

On and on and on the charlatan figures of so called authority, the do badder anointed ones, the ones who act and say as if they know best, surely, they know what they're doing because look at how grand their wisdom and success are. Look at how many yachts they have. Surely these are the smartest people on the planet. This is the best we have. These are the people to listen to. These are people to emulate and look up to. These are the people we should follow and defend and fight for. Even if it gets us nowhere let's do as they say. Because that's where we are. Worse, we are moving backwards. How convenient they don't go back to a tax rate that invested in society and helped us advance, all of us advance.

But they just can't share or give back at all. They make hundreds of times more than us but are not hundreds of times better than us. Their egos are as big as their fat greed guts, fucking monsters.

What have we really gotten from them in terms of progress?

p- So, what if some devices get smaller, faster, seemingly more complicated. It's not working. As a whole, what we are doing as sentient beings is not working out. All these things, big and small, cheap, or expensive, how's it going? Where are we going? What have we gotten ourselves into? How do we get out of it? Does any of it matter? Did it ever? What the hell are we supposed to do now? What is the plan? Somebody has got to have a plan that doesn't end in annihilation of the planet and all its occupants.

On and on and on the questions go and oh, yes. Fuck yes, they will sell you the answer. Snake oil in a bottle, a pill, a diet of misthoughts, misdeeds, misdirection, they sell you and your soul to the moon for a dollar and back again for a penny. They do this over and over and we keep letting them. We keep falling for it again and again. Dressed up differently here and there we do it thinking this time it will work. We will be happier, get what we deserve, get what we think we want this time because they put on lipstick but now want to tell you you are not even allowed to wear lipstick. Make up your fucking mind. Be proud and just tell us the plan to own us all and kill anyone that opposes dear leader.

Really, they are dressing you down, past your skivvies and past your soul so that one day, after they've pressed your face so deep into the mud, after they've stepped on your back so hard it breaks, after you try to look around but cannot see, but can hear the cries of your children, friends, and family around you, muffled crying in the mud, too. Then they move onto the next village, farm, town.

You think, just then you might die. Just then you might already be dead, for it is no life this impossible task they've put upon you. You were trained like a no conscience animal to obey. You followed their orders, and it got you not somewhere amongst the sparkles, not up there. You are filth and waste and meat to them.

You are somewhere though. You are down here, face fucking down in tear-drenched muck. Had enough. Ready to fight back?

Then they laugh. You cry harder. Then they rub shit on your hands and feet and tell you they're not done with you yet.

Now here's your chance. Yes, there might be another one someday but today you are in the mud. Do you continue to eat their mud pies, or do you eat Pie? Our Pie is different, it actually tastes good.

P- Begin anywhere that strikes you and go through the ways and means of Pie. Where, when, how is Pie?

p- Simple. You just have to feel your way through and in it.

P- That's it? What about all the other stuff it can do?

p- It's a lot.

P- What, Pie?

p- The responsibility.

P- To talk about it?

p- To know it. What it can do. All it can do. Everything about it.

P- What it will do?

p- What it is doing. If we get out of our own way. Just let it be. And be a good steward of Pie.

P- Is that likely?

p- Not in so far as history has shown.

P- What's to be done?

p- I've tried not trying. Leaving it to someone else. I mean if it really is that bad out there someone will do something. Won't they? They won't just let us continue to die and suffer en mass.

P- Isn't that exactly what they're doing?

p- I don't want the responsibility. It's not about me. It isn't about the progenitor of Pie either. They knew enough to step away.

P- Yet it takes people to make it work. Keep it going. What's the alternative? Let those with great wealth and power co-opt and corrupt its nature?

p- But not its core. Not if we strengthen it.

P- And how is that achieved?

p- By working together.

P- What is missing in this moment to achieve this end?

p- What is it always?

P- A reason?

p- A story. Narrative gives meaning.

P- And the story of Pie?

p- Today?

P- Let's think about how to grow it for tomorrow. What's missing in the plot?

p- Or too much of.

P- Sub-plot distraction?

p- It's mostly mechanics, money, and fallible boring people regaling us with their good time luck success. Too much look at me. It's losing the plot through creepy me me shit. Then a bone or two is picked or pricked about, having to do with the scope of Pie, tossed out like oxygen in between a swallow. But mostly there are money making schemes around it and you have no guide and no idea who to trust. There is no call center to get customer assistance from. To each their own. Spread the gospel, skip the sermon.

P- Like?

p- All the ways it helps poor people.

P- Doesn't it?

p- Not through tokenism. If these fuckers gave a shit about poor people, they wouldn't be so rich. Never mind their egos.

P- Aren't Pie's functions what make it useful and therefore appealing to someone unfamiliar with it?

p- Yes.

P- So?

p- It is more. So much more. It's an idea. People aren't going to rush to just an idea. It needs a context. It is gift glue not gum.

P- Aren't they spreading the word?

p- The message is hollow.

P- How do you get more to see?

p- And before it's too late.

P- Yes. Now how?

p- How do I show you what I see, what I know to be true? It's faith in the possible. Faith in the goodness of us overcoming the badness of them. It's too good to be true. How do you get them to trust you in a trust-less system where every word is a broken promise or abandonment of decency? Backed only by the glittering magnitude of putting us in a corner and acting surprised when we don't like it and want to rebel.

P- But do you rebel?

p- Pie is rebellion.

P- Is it how you get to ungreed?

p- Ungreed and Pie?

P- Do you think it might?

p- I think it just might.

P- And that is scary?

p- And exciting. But yes, I am afraid to believe. To be distracted by its component of greed. To allow that faith is enough.

P- Isn't this life stressful already?

p- Then why not try?

P- Then why not try?

p- Isn't there more to lose?

P- Is there?

p- But I might gain, we might all gain?

P- And you might succeed in sailing that sinking boat off a cliff to a better vista?

p- Ok, so fuck it. Let's go.

19

P- What the fuck?

p- Yep.

P- The news?

p- No matter.

Though, even if you tune it out, the evil seeps into your veins through the cracks of fast and easy non consensus reality. A pall hangs over glances and exchanges lost to the edge lost to time.

P- Is consensus reality a concession?

p- Be grateful for this gruel, they say. That fiction is not reality, we say.

P- Do they promulgate a just get over it mentality?

p- They push an I don't understand your logic, you are too emotional, stupid, naïve to understand narrative. It is a bedtime story for the already dead. There is always money for war but never money for milk, honey, books, or booze. Die they say. Not before we milk you of all your money and time. Barren robbers.

P- Wine is a luxury. Vacations, intimacy, healthy food, warm clothes, soft blankets, medicine, toys, paid utility bills, an education, not getting shot while you attend church, school, a parade, take a jog, are all luxuries. Aren't you to give those up?
p- How dare we have comfort and care. After comfort, everything else is distraction to keep you pacified.

Their disease has an off-shoot disease manifesting itself as despair. Completely avoidable and with a known cure they will never ever administer without greed being made to go extinct.

A vice is calories, comfort, and escapism. Those should never be qualified. Remember, we are supposed to be free to do what we want. The why and how come vast bodies succumb to booze and it's relatives are a lack of choice. No one chooses to die that way. These miseries are a symptom of their great power and wealth. Their success trickles down as a needle or a bullet. We are not at a picnic and their arsenal is vast. Duck and cover your lover, thoughts and prayers don't care about your feelings, they say. Tools of the trade, they say. Notice how their hands are callous free but not clean, I say. Bullies only think they want a fight.

It's the loss of each other and sense of being. From hunter gatherer tribe based, to do it alone mentality. We're told we're tribal but how are we really working together to make anything better versus getting even with people we're told to not like because it's their fault there is moral and societal decay. Stop feeding the fat fucking goose and see that the herding narrative is distraction 101.

P- It's the right time. Right place. And I'm the only person that has the ideas, training, and brilliance to do this. I'm the reason for any and every person to do this. Does that make sense?

p- You are the professor. Not me us is forward not back.

P- Well then, I tell every pupil, don't focus on the outside voices telling you what to do. Dance from the inside, for the inside. Not the external. If things were better, we wouldn't need to escape.

I also warn them of stochastic terrorism and tell my students to ask yourselves, will no one rid me of this meddlesome priest?

p- So that I might stay sucking rosaries but really be asleep. Not informed of and by any of it. I and you, both of us black sheep.

20

P- Did they groom you out of your senses?

p- The result was, desperation does not make for mild dispositions. They call me mad, and they are right. I am fucking mad as fuck.

P- The elimination of difference is the homogenization of culture. It is easier to fleece, I mean, police, the masses if conformity is in place. See something different and we are trained to rat out that different someone. To be gaslit, brainwashed, manipulated, is evil. Should we all just run away and join the circus?

p- Thank you for reminding us it's ok to be weird. For giving us permission. Except, I don't feel weird anymore. Pie helped me see that they are the aberrant ones. Billions of us getting along and a mere scab of them gorging all the billions for themselves. Mountain versus mole hill is doable. We got this. Pie opens eyes.

P- It is hard to imagine a fair scene for all. Many have fallen for evil dripped in their ears for years. There is a gap to overcome. There are difficult conversations to be had. There is an incredible credible

amount of work to be done. Just when you think you are making waves, they will push your head under, drowned followers will bite you. Sickness for miles and miles for many. The journey is an undertaking where gradually then suddenly a horizon shows.
With Pie, each Pie seer is a doer and a leader. In order to get where we are going, green grass on both sides, clear blue water all around, clear sky above, we are going to step on toes. What do we say to those we've hurt or might inadvertently hurt along the way?

p- This is a song with a melody stuck in the head, back when radio played the same music for all of us but only some of us got to hear it. Let us hear it together so we might dance this dance together.

Sorry I spoke at you, through you, to you like I couldn't see you. It's true not to quote you- if what you say is true- no, yes, it's true all right. I didn't see you for what you are, who you've become, what you've been, well I do now and I'm sorry now and then and for the future end of your reading this.

And then there was Pie.
And now here is Pie.

The bit part of Pie is going to keep making people jealous they can't have more of it. Time to go with crumbs, for we are crumbling. Not fractured which implies two or a few parts intact that brought back together would make a whole. No, we are fucking falling apart. Crumbling like a dead cathedral. Pie is finite but we are infinite. We are the more that will drive them to ground. Yes, Pie is fungible, but we are unique and priceless.

P- Why not use the known name then?

p- The biggest piece of evidence that Satoshi was human, is in naming the thing as if it were just a thing. This was impotence to not conceive a name as big and all-encompassing as something unknowable yet familiar because it is erudition in a down to earth manner. Pie is Déjà vu, without loo to loot. The ones who created this mess are not creators. They are limited and jealous of our powers. Why are we still listening to those that got us into this pit? They have had thousands of years to get it right, from soap and plumbing we are not far along on the advancement side of things. The name is limiting. And not delicious. As they succeeded in dumbing down the population- nuance, sarcasm, irony, and critical thinking are in short supply. Using one of their words, around their mismanaged market of soiled soul sucking thievery is why we steal the word for ourselves and rename it for ourselves and a yummier union. Doing the same thing over and over again is not sane. People are being left out. Let's let them in on the secret and joy and scrumptiousness of Pie. Pie is juicy deep pink watermelon sucked on a summer day. Also, the old name goes straight to the fucking money anti-thought side of things. Kill money and eat Pie.

P- And to those attached to the number of Pie, to getting a certain amount of Pie, filling their bags with Pie?

p- We'll never have a whole Pie but that's ok. That leaves a goal. Something to strive for that we will eventually not remember striving for long before we get anywhere near the end but really just the beginning of that empty ass goal. If you were doing Pie's work, you would not have bags of it. You would have used it to help others and not just yourself. Being selfish is so boring.

Remember, our aim is to not be a host shitting in the woods, in a pond, in a parking lot owned by another evil glass and steel and concrete eating sucking fucker. Our goal is total transformation.

A class at war does not have time to waste looking in the mirror.

P- I am afraid they will not let you pass go. Now what?

p- We are not asking for permission. You don't steal great power and wealth and get to be celebrated for it. Stop talking and show me you care.

P- The greed virus is a feeling. How do you stop a feeling?

p- We feel for each other and find value in each other, and they have nothing valuable. Monsters do not have feelings.

P- When we work together, we achieve peace. Greed is war. Is that so?

p- We have a common denominator to unite around.

P- Do we have to give anything to get everything?

p- Your labor is value. They die without your showing up not to do Pie's work but their dirty work of accumulating. Stop it.

P- Does Pie end the pain?

p- Our happening is not a war of yesterday. It is a conflict of will, action, and inaction. It is a bloodless event but not victimless.

P- Isn't this just profit of a different name?

p- We are beyond the self now; the work now is for others. We are a new kind of host. We feed off their greed to motivate us to spread empowerment to make things better not worse. We do not step over hurt people. We do not blame them for falling down, needing a hand, some heart. We pick them up and help them. Only in helping others do we help ourselves.

P- Many moves to be made?

p- Not really. There is no we'll make more to give us more and you less because you are less. There is but one, Pie.

22

P- Is Pie time affluence?

p- The term affluenza is a portmanteau of affluence and influenza, defined as a painful, contagious, socially transmitted condition of overload, debt, anxiety, and filth, resulting from the sick many legged dogged pursuit of more. A silly word created to express cultural disdain for consumerist waste haste. Though often used in jest, the term may contain more truth than many of us would like to know. Another greed virus symptom. Pie heals. Not Pie steals.

P- We know that, and when something is wrong, not fair, or does not feel right or just, how do we explain it to others?

p- It is a virus that mutates the empathy gene into an asshole gene.

P- Who will they attack to stop the healing?

p- They always go after truth seekers, tellers, artists, comedians, creative thinker types first.

P- Where are the leaders?

p- Societies produce some class leaders which in turn produce suck followers, suck political movements follow. We follow each other.

P- And impotent rage?

p- Pie connects people. Pie is meant for sharing. Pie is fruit.

P- Ok, so starting today, I, what?

p- Name them and shame them through public condemnation. Celebrate each frisson, you deserve it. Churches everywhere, nowhere is god.

P- Next?

p- Proselytize a future with and without Pie.

P- What does that do?

p- We break the wall of silence and get into the streets to teach, to make them hear, listen to the truth of Pie. Never bowing down to the disease of greed. Their reign of violence made victorious by your submission. That ended the moment you opened up.

P- What does one need to be?

p- Not a poet or a prophet alone. Prophets all of us and we are a cacophony too loud to silence.

The message is key. Not what it can do for you. What you can do, must do to raise consciousness of voice and purpose to lift us from reverie and misery money free. To be money done as a society.

P- What is the strategy?

p- Conquer. Tell them a story. Make it your own.

Survival of the Greediest

By p.

This is the story of empire. Very nearby, too close for comfort really, in a land ruled by sick evil fucks, er, I mean, foxes; a land that claimed to be the freest land in all the lands far and wide, lived two main types of animals- foxes and hens. On the backs of hens, this majestic land grew to be an empire. The lords of empire and supposed freedom were foxes. The foxes made the rules and controlled everyone and every resource in this land. They kept many hens too dumb to question the fox's motives. They told those hens it was the other hens that kept nice things just out of their reach. Even though the bulk of the land was inhabited by hens with common fucking sense, what they wanted did not matter. The monarchist foxes loved them some empire freedumb land. But not the vassal hens. Oh so many beautiful, dignified hens just wanting to go about being nice, kind, playful hens but the foxes wouldn't let them. The foxes were a weak impure nasty lot and soon a rot set in, and the land of empire turned foul by greed, envy, and wickedness. The hens did not control anything and scratched through dirt to get food and shelter. Poor poor hens in a rich rich land. In this land, one fox's poor choice might keep them poor in a moment. One hen's poor choice kept them poor in perpetuity.

This land was a nation of rich foxes on top and poor hens on the bottom. The disparities in empire freedumb land grew to the point where .01% of the foxes controlled more power and wealth than all of the hens and even most foxes combined. Soon, this was no longer the land of hopes and dreams but materialistic gladiator style competition with only a few winners and mostly poor or ever dwindling gullible middleclass losers, for they thought one day they too could be a fox. But even middleclass hens were getting squeezed by the pathological greed of ultra-foxes. This nation of poor hens was the choice of haters, losers, and liars of fox nation. Foxes in power chose for hens not in power whether mechanisms for attaining riches or staying in poverty were accessible or not. It's no surprise fox politicians on the payroll of fox billionaires and big business used words like access- "access to healthcare" and choice- "school choice." A hen that likes to fish might have access to a yacht if they live by the sea, but that hen cannot choose to have that yacht if that hen does not have the fair market opportunities to afford that yacht. Ok, so the hens should've just made some opportunities happen, said the foxes with great wealth and power. They said it so often, like good propaganda, society began to say it too and parrot it back to all the hens as reality- if I'm not wealthy, which equals success, which equals power, then it must be my fault. Though policies, bribed and bought, made it all but impossible for but a few hens to ever break out of their socioeconomic animal class. The hen's wings were clipped. The foxes wore minks.

You have what was once colloquially known as rugged individualism for the poor, socialism for the rich. Today it is known as oligarchy, or everywhere greed breeds forever plan. Since at the same time they are making policy to keep you down, they are gluing policies in place and funneling their chosen judges into seats to keep those policies enacted and expanding to keep the rules biased in their favor forever and ever.

Back to the story. The foxes told the hens to choose at the feed box and vote for whoever they thought should rule the land. Well, the foxes learned from an old timer bigoted fox how to gerrymander the land so the foxes got to pick which hen votes would count all the while they told the uneducated hens that this is what voter integrity looks like. Actually, it was fox affirmative action for would be pale yellow chicken (sorry chickens) livered racists. The mama hens faired a similar fate. Mama could be hens didn't have bodily autonomy. Groups the foxes deemed different, or trouble were made to fear life, limb, and liberty.

P- Sorry for interrupting the story of empire, tell me how this is freedom land again?

p- No problem. You cannot have the fox guarding the hen house without a lot of hens getting eaten. Unhappiness is a result of imperial state sanctioned greed. This is a conspiracy. More than two foxes are involved in conspiring to keep hens from flying. The state of affairs is not deep, not at all. It is shallow like a fox. Eventually, all the hens died of sadness and starvation, even in the richest and most prosperous of lands, and the foxes died because they couldn't figure out how to work a can opener on their own. The end.

P- It sounds familiar. I think I know this land. Here, I have one.

The Pie Makers Revenge

By P.

Not long ago in a not far off place there was an entity known as The Pie Maker. The Pie Maker seemed to be a regular sort of sort. Watching banks do messy business preoccupied The Pie Maker. After the banks got one too many bail outs, one day, The Pie Maker cleverly recognized humans insatiable appetite for more and decided to do something about it. Pie was born as a project from the projects of human potential and yearning for more. This project resulted in a clever bit of math, so called number go up technology that ensured the survival of Pie in its nascent days. Pie would stretch through all of slave society as a means of freeing people from their enslavers. For Pie to reach a level of saturation in society that brings about hyperpieization, what a tasty high that will be, more than greed must be introduced and cultivated by Pie friends and allies. This too is a canny, though only recently apparent, feature of Pie. The Pie Maker saw that humans could not be trusted to do the right thing as long as greed was a dominant characteristic of the ruling class. By removing themself from any leadership role in the adoption of Pie, The Pie Maker built in an unspoken contract, much like the blockchain it's built on, and is developed around. Yet, instead of technology alone doing the work of ensuring two parties fulfill an obligation, it is people that must step up and have each other's backs to realize this fairer future. A harder lift to be sure as evidenced by the current winner take all, capitalism or bust, profits over people, war over peace current mentality rich greedy inhumans have built and codified into the very being of what a great then, now, supposedly civilized society should be versus the story of Pie. The end?

p- You cannot work Pie into the existing corrupt system and hope for a different outcome. Move over, it's our time.

P- I can't even fathom a world where I would purchase a second yacht while I have employees that work multiple jobs and are on government assistance just to make ends meet. These are the welfare originators. What the fuck is wrong with people?

p- It's disgustingly atrocious. Greed ate my soul, let's eat yours.

I used to have questions around the concept of choice and how false it is. Thinking we are a collection of decisions made by us and imposed on us by systems functioning just as they were designed to do. Like being corralled into a pen for slaughter but given a view along the way. Told and made to believe by corporate media propaganda along the way that if we only study harder, work harder, vote harder we too can live the dream myth and have the myth dream life. It is a lie of course. This lie that anything is possible, not statistically true. Another misdirection propagated by corrupt politicians and a sold out fourth estate.

P- What is the Pie long game?

p- Not a game, life. Real good life worth living.

P- Does doing the honorable thing matter?

p- Only fighting battles you know you can win is a sure way to lose. Doing the right thing matters.

P- A Pie eating competition would spread attention, education, and excitement about Pie. What are some other things to be done?

p- Why don't some of these Pie whales do a national give away of Pie to garner awareness and excitement and hope, like state lottery systems where people spend hard earned money on a prayer?

P- Or establish traveling schools to learn about Pie. They could be remote pop-up schools in rural and inner-city areas. Doable?

p- Or actually pay people in a national or international sort of job works program to learn about Pie and get wide-ranging proselytizing under way. Like an old-time tent revival ministry.

P- Or Pie protagonists do a debt jubilee for some group, town, or segment of the population that has an issue. Charitable Pie style?

p- People want to work, be useful, feel valuable. Why not a literal Pie works project? Put people to work building Pie infrastructure. Solutions should not be driven by a tacky profit incentive.

P- I charge every new Pie booster to be bigger and better than those who came before. Pie for Pie's sake. Why not?

p- We've got to stop measuring success by how many zeros follow one's name. The strangeness that they don't even really have that money (paper money meet paper tiger) as such that they actually get bailouts, tax credits, subsidies, and refunds from the government. What the fuck is wrong with these monsters? These are morally bankrupt sick fucks. They are weak loser inhumans.

P- The same mistakes of dying empire systems and glorifying status through wealth is repeating itself. To these greed virus infected assholes, how many fucking whole Pies do you need?

p- Alas, they need all of it because, you know, money. Money is power and they are weak melting snowflake servants to evil. We will die at their greedy pasty little hands if we don't figure out a way to collectively say- nope. No fucking way will I pay. You are not going to pillage me or anyone, thing, plant, or ocean again.

They have so much great power and wealth they are so bored.

P- How bored are they?

p- They are so bored and traitorous to the human race they want to leave earth on phallic shaped rocket ships. Jerk offs jerking off on trips to space, the so obvious it's not even ironic sightseeing imploding submersible trips in the sea to gawk at the once great sunken titanic vessel, and literal cage matches between one billionaire and another. Let's call it now. Ban billionaires. Pathetic pricks playing tricks wishing they had micks and thick swallows to rub together instead bouncing our wombs, our bodies, ourselves.

P- What do you call a kind billionaire?

p- Daisy food?

P- Not a billionaire?

p- They are anti-us and we are anti-them.

P- Let us go gently into that sweet and savory Pie night, right?

p- Being overwhelmed by Pie is like hearing about lottery winners who blow all their money. You have to have been raised without money and go through it to understand it. There's the shame of how I could let this happen and echo of I'll never be so lucky/ irresponsible. It's a lot like receiving love. The heart has to be open to the process. You cannot accept what you do not believe.

P- Small steps like these?

p- A child becomes a giant becomes a behemoth. We need a plan.

P- We build a 42-year plan like the anti-everything good assholes?

p- Yep. Good comes for evil and prevails, winded sails nailed. Tick tock, next block.

23

P- People love money more than people. True or false?

p- Some people don't want to be left alone.
It's cultures deep.
It's a bit of superfluity.
Bit by bit, bye byte, bite by night.
Breathe before you forget how and why.

P- Is that your answer?

p- It's a trick question.

P- So you have a trick answer?

p- I'm tired of playing. I need a nap. We all need a nap.

P- Life is not a game though, is it?

p- That's right.

P- Are you going to answer the question?

p- Of course it is true.

P- Of course?

p- The proof is empirical. We see and experience the evidence every day. I've been trying for years, decades, hours that don't exist, working mind to the bone trying to make sense of it. It's senseless.

P- That's just the way it has to be?

p- It's why my head and gut hurt all the time.

P- Shouldn't you just get over it? Especially now, as an adult?

p- When I was a child my belly ached often. Sometimes it was from hunger. Food being a reward for doing good and right. When it wasn't hunger outright from a physical lack of nourishment, it was an insatiable reckoning to understand the emptiness I felt. To reenforce feeling anything.

P- As a child you had no words for it. As an adult the words don't satisfy either. They're only half truths. Are they even?

p- Half or true?

P- That was the question. True or false?

p- The answer is also false.

P- Because now you're an adult?

p- Because there are still hungry children.

P- Ah, the deep duplicity arises. Going to solve world hunger, are you?

p- Not one of us alone. This is Pie adjacent territory. What is hushed on about in circles too small to be heard by the masses.

P- If they only knew the answer was here already?

p- You mock?

P- No. I smile at the treachery. If only they knew what was coming for them?

p- They do. Too late.

P- How can you be so sure?

p- Because children are still hungry. The double speak is not as effective as it once was. This is a moment of greatness and a great many seeing. Our tools are still hidden from us though. Pie came along and relied on that greed, generational greed, gaming us for generations. To keep it going they rely on us not learning. It is an evil to encourage ignorance. They are bullies and simple thieves.

It is a weakness on their part. The few of them. Alone or together their numbers are small. Ours grow with each passing crumb of Pie. The problem of greed, wanting more Pie than you can afford or eat alone is a remnant of the old time.

My belly still hurts not because of time's betrayal but from the duality phase we are going through, had to go through, to make a new world where there is no great hunger, no great power of the old sort, no great wealth. No cognitive dissonance, true is true.

P- The dichotomy grows lopsided. Too heavy not to fall over. I've seen this before. Not quite this, with Pie in the mix now. But this toppling of empire at their own hand. Unfettered greed getting the best of the basted of their day. Days numbered over and over. An inevitable countdown only to be repeated again and again.

The Pie is already mostly divided though. How can the remaining Pie crumbs be enough?

p- And so we return to the numbers. It's math it is. Bendable math that does not lie. Pie is not just about the math it is about math that is infallible when left alone. It does not lie, it does not take more that it's fair share, it is not weak of mind and spirit. It does not abuse and oppress those that have the least power and resistance.

P- And the exceptions to the rule?

p- But for math. Only people. They try to fool us people with that bullshit.

P- Let's clarify what the bullshit is, yes?

p- Easy. That Pie is money about money for, to, and how to make money. Ugh. So plebeian all this money obsession. Limiting and for the incurious, intellectually lazy, and intellectually dishonest.
P- Go away and experience the world for yourself and not for what they tell us it is. Learn about other people, cultures, lands different than your own. A lack of exposure to other ways of being keeps your mind small and sheltered. Then return to where we're from to share what we've learned. You don't need money to experience the world. Read books. As many as you can from as many different

authors as you can and learn about place and perspective. Or else. Money suffocates. Money is lack of empathy and wearisome righteousness instead of untiring appreciation and unfaltering humility. Do we return to where we began?

p- Through reading more. Lots more. Look, listen, learn.

P- Read what they tell you?

p- Sure. Then read what they tell you not to read. Silly twats, afraid of books. Because of course they are. Books are magic and they are afraid of witches.

P- Read anything and everything. If they tell you it must be banned, read especially those books. And books are better than snipped clip words that flash by. Who paid for those words and thoughts but the machine you protest against. A book is a holistic interactive act relying on you. Can they burn all the books in time?

p- The deadline again. Well, time is running short because the puss filled minds of the weak ass bully babies have swirled demons among us, uneducated victims really, to swarm gates of history and critical thinking. They have made much progress and continue to multiple as any virus is wont to do.

Replicate but don't fornicate, something like that. Immaculate conceptions for mass dunces, something like that. Cut the cord. A book is not a paper weight, best not to wait longer than you must. Tick tock, next block.

P- But maybe they just want to be different like everybody else?

p- It's a shame. Our shame is misdirected. Shame them. Be yourself. Be a nice fucking person. Stand up and fight for someone you don't know. Judge the executioner, not the jury.

P- Is this a revolution?

p- Oh, so war and things like them? With or without blood?

P- In the classical sense?

p- In the primitive old time old way they did it before and continue to use war against their own people sense. War is never civil.

P- War is what bullies do in the name of protectionism, trite, eh?

p- Boring yes. Dead babies are not trite, no. Their money motives are scary stupid wanna be might and white as a ghost frightening.

P- The Pie maker understood the beckoning for a leaderless movement. Yet, there is a natural inclination to organize and rally around one person, one theme, if it is not revolution, what is it?

p- I feel like somebody is going to get me for having these thoughts. For all the thoughts I've had before. For all the acts I did and did not do. Our heroes never live up to expectation, we look for them anyway. Or so it has seemed.

P- Is the difference that they now know they are not heroes? By design, by ego, by influence, and not reluctant? Not relevant?

p- Anyone claiming to know what is going on is an idiot.

P- So what do we know?

p- We know we are all gonna die. There is virus spreading like wildfire, this virus is greedy. Fortunately only a small percentage of the world's population has the full-blown version of this virus. Unfortunately it is air and lack of thought born contagious.
P- How do we achieve health and harmony as sickness abounds?

p- We, right now, poof, done. This happening is happening. We stop competing, yes, we still have incentive but no more war.

P- Pie helps to destroy empire?

p- In this moment we just saved a little more Pie, a little more Pie was equally distributed in thought and deed by just us being here.

P- Pain does not equal gain, what does not kill you makes you more grateful for crumbs?

p- Fuck no. Of course pain hurts. Of course seeing others in pain hurts. That is the difference between them and us. We're not monsters. Grateful is a problematic concept. A bit of gaslighting going on with that one. I don't owe them shit. They owe us.

P- I am disturbed by their insatiable appetite for greed and murder. I do not know if words or happenings will be enough, will they?

p- I'm quite furious at the people in charge, and strive to, in even just a small way, move the needle of imbalance so that the people not at the top of the ladder have more of a vote in how and why societies form and function. What you pay attention to grows.

P- Then it is conclusive. Pie is happening and we grow or shrink?

p- I have a stomachache.

P- Is it too much to digest?

p- Eat the rich and more Pie.

P- There is no other way?

p- It's the only way. The world is broken. Money is the root cause. Money is indisputably evil. Those with great wealth and power are greedy and hoarding wealth to a pathological level never encountered amongst humans. They are destroying the planet for continued human tweedle dumb. They must be stopped.

P- An intervention? A happening?

p- Immediately. We've already wasted too much time. Too much unnecessary suffering at the hands of psychopaths. It's misery incarnate. Things are not getting better, more chill, just ask earth.

P- Pie will end moral turpitude?

p- No, but it interrupts it. We end the violent depravity of the systems currently in place. We are the weapon. We are the answer. It's unsustainable insanity, what we are doing now.

P- Happenings on earth, around Pie, is going to fix all that?

p- Not just physically. Pie is just the vessel. We use our spirit. This is a spiritual crisis. The structures in place are convenient distractions and lazy excuses for preventing a remedy based on humanity's infinite capacity to rise up and slay the sickness greed.

P- Without the humanities we are lost. Our moral compass corrupted by vapid bright colorless yearning. The squawking and the yelling are brainwashing methods to make us go numb, tune out instead of turn up. We read to learn about the way things were so we can grow. Stay enraged but then make happenings so?

p- One moment at a time. Tick tock, next block.

P- How else is gaslighting used?

p- I have a headache.

P- Are we back here again?

p- It's the only way through.

P- What gaslighting tactic can be turned back onto them?

p- It would go something like- Wanted: Ungreed.

P- And?

p- All others do not apply.

P- And?

p- Ok, backing up real quick. Don't be seduced by power and greed yourself. Focus, cut it out, it is not a shortcut.

And then we apply pressure, everywhere all the time. Most of them are still capable of being shamed but you have to get creative about it and be just as merciless as they are in your naming and shaming them. Do not idolize or celebrate them. Rank them. They are so weak and rank. They humiliate us publicly and privately; they will not stand up so well under the pressure of bombastic naming and shaming. They crave adoration like a dog.

We cast them out like pariahs or lepers of old, because let's be real, they are. A leper, most often due to poverty, caught their illness. Because we, as a society neglected them. Those with great power and wealth are referred to as filthy rich. This is fitting. Instead of endowing them with titles of prestige like the first, second, or third, reminding us of how many generations have passed by while we were busy not stopping them. We do not actually live in a meritocracy, and most did not get that way by merit. To say they earned their fortunes, is to give them credit undeserved. Often starting with a leg up, the system is intentionally designed to help them and not others, kind of like that style of government they are always accusing us of wanting. You know, the one where the government runs everything. Like the revolving doors of wealth, power, privilege, blood smoked rooms and smoke-stained calls for fairness and justice. Only for thee not me. Libertine liberty killers. We need to see them anew, in light of Pie.

P- We shall instead see them for what they are- hoarding parasites manipulating the host populace to ever feed their toxic skanky ways. We have been distracted and have not held them to account. A rabid animal will act until it is stopped and given medicine. If these evil beasts are to be cured, they must be contained and quarantined. The ones that do not make it shall better fertilize the earth they have callously and causally poisoned with their greed. Our happenings are easy enough then, many people already do this. So, step up the shaming?

p- But you are more than just a troll. You have other powers too.

P- Humor is an effective way of bringing them down?

p- Laugh at them fierce. It bothers their boiled lizard brains. They think they are strong and tough, but they are weak bullies. They are precious with their preachiness claims to what is ours by birth, self-determination, by land, or by sea, or air, or spirit. They rob our souls; we must rob their souls. Resources once stolen are being returned, starting now. Now we add labor boycotts.

P- Public and private strikes, too?

p- Boycotts, strikes, uprisings of a classic sort. Make them play whack a mole with our lives and labor, they already do, this time do it with Pie in mind. Remember, Pie is their money killer. Money kills, we kill their money. Withhold your labor, withhold your consent, withhold your money, they can't do shit without their slaves.

P- Can you imagine them picking their own strawberries or cleaning their own toilets?

p- Nice picture. All of these are happenings. It is happening now.

P- This is a pandemic?

p- We've already had the practice. Do not fall into an information silo. Channel your temper. Apply your zealotry to where it counts.

P- What exactly is the happening?

p- Us, Pie, doing everything and anything to upset the paradigm.

24

P- Why wealth?

p- If the system is so great, why are so many people failing at it?

P- Wealth does not create health. Are you the reluctant hero?

p- So now I have to clean up their mess? No, not me. All of us.

P- Just thinking about it makes you a hero?

p- Just thinking about it means it is happening, so here we go.

P- How does Pie foster ungreed when there is only a finite amount if it? Doesn't it bring out more more greed gimme mine behavior?

p- Pitfalls are built into this beginning crawl before you can walk stage. The smash and crash for more cash stage was and continues brutally to be sure. Monetary rewards came to those clever with faith and patience. Yes patience. This is base layer crust Pie. We are in it for the filling so that we establish a future so filled we don't rely on old base layer versions of wealth, power, and success as equaling health and happiness. That is the old way. Pie is now.

P- If they're not going to get rich, how do you make them care?

p- As one begins to step out of the toxic echo chamber and read and learn and listen, one begins to see that place of no discerning sharp greedy edges. We are over here. Pie is bigger than that.

P- Who will soften the edges?

p- Who can risk it, you mean?

P- Everyone but them and even the theys of them that feel this is not right. Fight right. Too right. We believe in right and wrong, truth and lies, reality not condemned reality. Come for the money stay for the message if you must but be careful. Fear is here?

p- Fear is the culprit. We have ceased being relevant as individuals in the pantheon of greed feed dictated to us from above by those with great power and wealth. There is other shit happening in the world. We can stop being dependent on corporations running us.

P- Solution and problem- Pie is a connection already begun and well grooved into much consciousness. That hook it has placed in many eyes and hearts, it has also, almost too much and too late, anchored the greed. How so?

p- Problem in search of a solution is their modus operandi. You know the problems they never solve but create and then blame some other group for. With technology advancing, they cultivate quicker and sturdier ways to keep you, the rabble, numb, dumb, and out.

P- But aren't they still playing catch up because Pie was born from the bottom up, the way of any good happening?

p- Mad, as they are, that we had dibs to it and took it upon ourselves to grow it, they now want to stop that access from getting too democratic, because they hate people power, unless they get a bigger piece of the Pie. Never forget their motives are impure. Evil to be sure.

P- But the bigger Pie gets, the closer we get to full Pie and farther from the current system, no?

p- There is still much to do in between that has nothing to do with old time money. And much they want to keep between us and Pie, like their old time monied ways. To keep the focus on the monetary side of it keeps it in their system lane of control and limited access. Just thinking and living Pie hurts their system.

P- The early days of wonder and excitement and yes, profit is now diminished. As anything new and shiny begins to fade, the mystery is still marred by how not to get broke or broken by the sometimes often brutally steep learning curve. It can instead be enough to celebrate and teach Pie before we can even reach for any Pie for ourselves. In the acts of expanding awareness and reach for others we grow in our own proximity to the potential of ourselves and Pie. We make it stronger just by caring and sharing its energy.

The gobbledygook of all this rings like a duck's platitudes. They can fly, you know?

p- Right. They are not just hopping around and stuff. We with water lilied emotions and sentiment. Just start feeling it and don't be too cute like a bird, that is the entryway? Trust but fly.

P- Those on the inside, Pie's big defenders have always been its biggest beneficiaries. To fold in a next generation, with its intimidating unit price, the price of entry must come down and be accessible in another way. How does such a way come about that is cheap and easily afforded en masse but feels expensive enough to make it desirable?

p- Sell it as a spiritual salvation but not the hypocritical kind.

P- Won't religion as opiate of the masses be off putting for those not fallen or susceptible to hierarchical authoritarian structures?

p- This is why Pie's communal, not libertarian, nature is stressed, harnessed, and elevated as the paramount source of its power.

P- For it is in community that great power and wealth is actually felt and received versus the selfish lonely islands of one?

p- While the work is being done, there is the likelihood many will be flooded off the diminishing shores of me me island.

P- To rely on big nature is to forego the accumulative effects of each little human coming together to sentence them to solitary forever. As forever is a long time, even farther as a time away, they have given you no choice in the matter. Therefore, the out loud cry is to pick up the gauntlet before too long has come. Will words and bodies do?

p- Through Pie?

P- Next to Pie. Along with language and through the physical and psychological protest that is Pie, you are nearly there. Here?

p- We will care about others and widen our circle of compassion. That does not include me caring if you get a helipad for your yacht, rather, in a decent society, you don't get to have a yacht until everyone has a full belly and a safe warm place to lay their head at night. I don't sleep. You don't sleep.

P- Can you pray your way to being a better human being?

p- The opposite price of becoming a truly conscious species?

P- A human being exists in time and space and is part of a whole. One cannot help but see themselves as distinct from all the other parts of the universe. One wants to feel important, special. When you only focus on yourself, your image of the world is reduced. As your knowledge yard gets smaller and turns inward, so does your place in the world. We naturally struggle with the inside outside parts of ourselves and our place in the universe. When powerful forces, those with great power and wealth, orchestrate an increase of separation between you, others, and time, you are enslaved. Your mind is not your own. Your body follows. They are escalating the attacks moment to moment, filling the noise with more noise. How do you follow the signal of plural self?

p- You become a void to be emulated and feared. Thoughts become words become actions become being become Pie manifest.

P- Develop consciousness of our role in a caste system. We are nothing more than resources for the monsters of a class system. Being informed and aware is central to waking up and rising up to the inhumanity waged against us. We should never get used to the idea that we are no longer valuable souls but processable animals. To leave the feed lot is to be called what?

p- Satoshiism.

P- Named after The Pie Maker?

p- Or entity. Or plural.

P- The many?

p- The one at a time to become our many made manifold.

P- Of Pie this will do?

p- Of Pie we will be.

P- One?

p- As many, unto one purpose.

P- For the many?

p- For all.

P- Eat the rich, eh?

p- Absolutely.

P- Eat them real good?

p- Fuck yes. It's consensus compassion.

P- Nobody loves those with great power and wealth, they will not be missed. Compassion and empathy will replace evil and greed?

p- It's what we need more of. People are in so much pain they are angry and afraid. Violent even, because of course they are. They are scared children emulating the lords of empire in freedumb greed land's crumbling kingdom. They are a symptom of all our undoing.

P- Weakest link and all that?

p- People are hurting and we do worse than nothing. For they have figured out ways to profit off the pain. Indeed, they relish in the pain while making vastly greater and greater sums of money, netting like a stuck fish, more resources. It is by choice, yet they act as if there was nothing else to be done. Gaslighting the way to owing it all. Controlling us all and still they have the nerve to tell us it is all our fault. Empty holiness shouted from the pulpit.

P- In the history of the world there have been few times the perpetrators face meaningful appropriate consequences for their dastardly actions. It is always and only after they have already committed crimes against humanity, time and time again. Will we never learn?

p- To say it is against nature supposes it is not in our nature. This is both correct and incorrect. It is in our nature by the very fact it occurs. They are a symptom. It is also in our nature to balk.

The vast majority of people are not such selfish assholes. We do not take lives for granted or hostages for profit. People want little more than the basics- food, shelter, health, and safety.

P- By intentionally making these human needs scarce, they pit people against one another. They drive our inner demons to the surface. We are so busy just trying to survive we forgive them their trespasses against good, god, and country. We have even been convinced by their lies that they deserve what they have, and we can and should want it too. If we are only better, faster, smarter, stronger. But should you want wealth and great power if it means death and destruction for the masses?

p- Only a monster infected with illness, a pathological greed virus, would want that. Otherwise it would make them a sick fuck if they did all this on their own.

P- For what?

p- Cruelty is the point. Small, mean, ugly, weak sick fuckers.

P- This trick is now happening with Pie. You are being told it is just a silly game of losses by losers while they build bigger games to get all the Pie profits. They can't stand the fact it came not from them above but from unknown beings below their reign of power. Someone or many someone's figured out something bigger than them and beyond their control. Now they are desperate to steel people against learning the truth while they steal what's left to be divvied. Is there enough time to bring Pie to everyone's table?

p- Not a full Pie. Fractions are what is available to most people. Though it feels out of reach at all if they can't have a whole one. Why bother, they say. The message must be spread that even just a bit of food on an empty belly is better than none.

If we are all cold and tired, just a bit of warmth and rest goes a long way. When our numbers grow, bit by bit, so does our strength and power. But it will not come going about it solo anymore. That is what got us into this mess. Touch grass, spread Pie inside out.

P- Previous peace movements failed. How do you get the people to unlearn the profit driven message of the last many millennia?

p- Exactly. Those movements were and are always corrupted by profit. These Pie happenings involve letting go of expectation of reward and doing it because it is a true thing to try after failing all other moments of change and upheaval. Incrementalism will not do. Whatever we have done and are doing is not working, is not enough. We will be radical in our approach and with it does come the benefit of being invulnerable to pressure or coercion.

But I get it. Greed is tough to resist. Especially when we see we have no real safety nets to speak of. Everyone just wants to protect themselves and their family. We will grow our family into a network spanning not just the globe but centuries of undoing all that garbage selfish hardwiring.

P- Regarding those born into a family dynasty of great power and wealth. We know their numbers are small compared to us. Do we end the diseased bloodlines of these few unfortunate souls?

p- Human energy. Mass bodies of untapped human potential and drive. Fully realized, we are a nightmare to their entire way of corruption and murder. We practice Pie to remake the world in the image of ungreed.

Not content to take all the wealth before Pie, as they come for all the rest of Pie now, it is in every day the message of Pie belongs.

Sharing all the patty cake baby Pie bits amongst ourselves is the way through, and up, and up, and above the evil. It is a slog of a journey. A task for reluctant heroes. The trodden cannot make it so we must make it for them. We do this not just for ourselves but those dear and far from us because it will spread good flames.

P- Once people know?

p- Yes, once people know, they fall down like the drunken fool too shit faced to believe the room is not really spinning. Not just the room, the world. It's the whole of humanity and all it is capable of. All of life turned on its head by unreal unrealized possibility.

P- It is too big, too true, too good to be true, most people are still too in the fog of great greed's influence to trust it. This problem of trust is part of what must be overcome. How do you get the trustless to believe?

p- Temptation worked in the begging but now we are at a new stage requiring new tools and a new message with new incentive.

P- Is there an unfortunately?

p- Yes. The mass psychosis must have an exit of unique meaning but shared purpose. Or shared meaning and unique purpose. Either way gets us the way.

P- We could fail?

p- Look at where we are now.

P- We don't really have a choice?

p- Sit on the sidelines and find out.

25

P- Are we talking about a healthy society vs. the sick one we currently live in but most of us don't see because we rationalize the horrors away based on the brainwashing we've had?

p- To put it simply, yes. To mention the housing deprived in the street, the drug addled, the mentally ill, the ill from mentalness, the children hungry, abused, treated as pawns in their sickness selfishness at all cost game, is to name the invisible. The could be mamas who do not have agency over their bodies in the name of a conjured white god of green greed excused by every excuse in a ballyhoo book because their innate power threatens cowardly venal devils of species dominance and degradation.

P- Or those working countless hours unable to get ahead or rest for a minute while they make more in a minute than the ungreedy net in a lifetime. Big game hunts little game, fun game, isn't it?

p- Life is not a game, politics is personal. Money is personal. Resources are personal. Those with great power and wealth fucking up everything beautiful is personal. Those with great power and wealth gaslighting the masses is personal, same as used agent orange on my heritage rhododendrons or heirloom tomatoes.

And now we get back to how Pie helps fuck their shop of evil closed forever. We won't need their guns and toys when we don't need their pretend money lies. It's not real. None of it was ever real. Occasionally one gets through, and they hold them up, see, it is a fair system. All lies. All a masquerade. Damn these bastards.

P- Pay attention to the everyday horrors whilst they distract with the big ones?

p- Use little pie to distract from big Pie. Little pie eventually eats big Pie.

P- When can they exist?

p- When all are fed, warm, and sheltered well. By then there won't be a them anymore and we will not desire such empty fillings.

P- They won't tolerate it. You're just a tool to them. A nobody vessel to lay down their great power and wealth on and around as they continue to rape, plunder, punish, and pillage, village to mind. This is the work of centuries. You are too smart to be so dumb?

p- Of course I am. And you now too.

Of course they went too far too long ago. Going overboard with the punish part. For all the gaslighting, even the poorest of poor, and us dummies, know it wasn't our choice to be born without great power or wealth. Being told we are weak, unworthy, undeserving, unanointed isn't working anymore. People may have been fooled but we are not fools and will not be made to play foolish with Pie left to their disposal of it too. Everything they touch dies. They hate us. They want to kill us. We are such a fucking bother for them to put up with. We are all going to die. Nobody is coming to save us. Nobody cares about you or me, not really, no one with the power to do anything about anything.

P- Trauma is what they have wrought. Punished for being born poor and all. Really, in the caste or not. For you cannot punish the lot for what station in life they were born at. And then, not everyone is going to want to climb a ladder to be a monster, too. Not a ladder. A rung on the ground and one overhead to remind you of what they have over you. It is quite sick and disgusting.

This is where they went wrong- thinking everyone will want the same big shiny nothings for nobodies but themselves. They overplayed their hand trying to make us feel bad all the time for the countless things not only not in our control but actively aggressively manipulated by them to keep us down. Then Pie?

p- Pie shows a way forward without them. And now, like fat little babies, they're crying mommy foul and having tantrums. These are not serious people. They have literally let the planet, the big fucking picture, slide towards entropy and they expect us to continue supporting their drip habit. Abusing, lying, hoarding, hovering over us with old and new technology to force their systems down our throats. We are not even with privacy to mourn.

P- My neck will not take their boot if you stand up. Look up and shout. Is that the to do?

p- Thundery loud.

P- Your numbers make you heard. Like with Pie?

p- Just like with Pie. The bitty pieces may feel and taste like mere crumbs. This might make you sad and greedy like them, at first, that you can't have more. You may even, likely, do greedy unkinds to yourself and others, things to get a bigger piece of Pie. This will result in pain.

P- How to avoid the pain?

p- For some there will be no going around it, they will go through it and may be too bitter on the other side and will give up on Pie.

Some will listen and learn. And learn to swim slow, then fast, and then slowly lovingly with the current. Eat fast swallow later.

The others, those that bound like bulls- there is no shame. You did nothing wrong. You moved when you should have stayed still. You trusted when you should have held your own. You may start again not from a bottom but a greater place of wisdom. It's ok. You're going to be ok. We all fuck up sometimes. You are ok.

P- Will you hold their hand?

p- Many hands holding each other will lift us through and above the greed. We will learn and discover together lightness over depths of despair.

P- And to those with great power and wealth? What does this say?

p- It says they are not welcome. They have never been wanted. Certainly not needed.

P- And now?

p- In fucking us over with unchecked unimaginable greed they fucked it for themselves. Not sorry for you mate. Cry harder.

P- Anything they can do to make it right?

p- They would have done it already if it was in their nature. Remember, these are sick individuals whose pathologies are destroying trees, souls, and bees to have more stuff. At any time, they could have fed children, fixed broken buildings, kept the air and water clean. Instead, they laughed while we cried. These evil monsters will not stop until we stop them.

P- They are taking us back. Empires always fall. Always. An empire in decay revolts like vomit, upon itself, doubling down on war and greed. This task for Pie is great. Pie as protocol may be up for it, are you?

p- Ha!

P- This is humorous?

p- It is. Many of my humors are flowing.

P- Is it a nervous laughter?

p- It was.

P- And?

p- Pie is a happening on reality. As it was once coerced and forced upon us.

P- Not anymore?

p- Not anymore. My nerves are alive.

P- What do we say to the watchers?

p- Dangerous evil liars are what they are. Murderous and corrupt. So dumb. What a waste of life. Of talent and energy. Disgorge yourself. And remember to breathe at night so you don't suffocate. That would be awful, you might not even make it to see Pie's success.

P- Will you be allowed to govern yourselves with ungreed or be ruled by a greedy minority?

p- That is the happening we have already begun. As long as many monsters do bad, we do good, the decision is done.

P- How do you stop the desperate from becoming dangerous?

p- You cannot meet people halfway on values. Either you care about people, plants and animals, or you don't.

P- Pie is the answer?

p- Every accusation is a confession. Pie is our return confession.

P- How do you like them crumbs?

p- What crumbs? They've poisoned the entire bake. You cannot coexist with monsters that do not see you as anything but fodder and prey. They are takers. We are makers and bakers. Bake pie.

P- Name please?

p- Criminal plutocratic elite.
Humanitarian crisis.
Abuse of power.
Overt vs. soft focus death cult.

P- What beauty needs protecting?

p- We protect who, what, where, when, why that needs protecting. We build beds not bunkers. We love and we see. And Pie is a world we choose to be.

Don't be clever. Be clever.
Pull the lever.
Pie.
Pie.
Pie.

Don't give up.

P- Puff pastry lamination?

p- Pie and a rolling pin.

P- That's it?

p- That's it. When you choose to care you are going to have your heart break. A lament. Decades caring. Many lifetimes dying. The hard fight too hard. The do or die. I did both and cried after each. Make them fight me. Go limp. Go heavy. Have big found plans with the big space filled with mere presence found by joy.

We were once told we take up a lot of space. It's not enough. The more more of Pie in thine eye is die die to the feed of greed.

Give up. Eat more pie. Don't try. It's Pie. It will take care of you if you care to do. You are seen. Be the mean. Don't get green. Ungreed is Pie. Full calorie fruit filling.

P- Facts or feelings?

p- Isolated.
Terrified.
Inadequate.
Traumatic.

Pie.
pie.
Stick it in your eye.
Pie.
Pie.
My.
My.
Yours.
Mine.
Pie.
Pie.
Pie.

P- Both?

p- Both.

P- Can Pie heal a sick society?

p- Pie allows for the transformation of individuals driven insane with worry about crumbs and feeling crumby to complete souls, driven and focused by selfless creation of a whole human organism, with all our messy interconnected parts, working for a clean, fair, math based, mode of being. A healthy versus insanity-based system working with, not against, a natural order of connectivity, energy, and planetary strength.

We shouldn't have jobs. Not as such, tied to our worth and value. The banker is not better than the baker. In fact, of course we know they are worse because they feed the greedy. Bakers feed souls.

P- We cannot continue to tolerate systems which must necessarily abuse workers with financial pain in order to keep increasing profits and quarterly statements. We must transcend these competition-based models where people are manipulated by financial pain into stepping on each other's heads in a rat race to show the ruling class that they can generate more profit for their employer than their neighbor can.

As we move into collaboration-based systems, where we all work together for the good of everyone, we and the planet will thrive. Our current status quo systems are choking us to death. How do we abstain from capitalism?

p- We opt out. With every choice big and small. We change our priorities to include less of the material and more of the spirit.

P- Are we thinking about it all wrong?

p- Not all wrong. I will try to be more declarative going forward. It's hard because I am mindful of being inclusive to whatever it is that draws someone to Pie.

P- It is not limiting?

p- Only by imagination. Imagination is dangerous.

P- Do we need to draw a bigger picture?

p- For more to see? Yes.

P- For more to believe?

p- Yes. And with the energy and eagerness like the young one who plays chess. Who is fearless in taking the picture off the board and into the world.

P- We are not bound by structure?

p- It informs. It guides. It also causes conformity and can refuse to bend.

P- Until it breaks that is?

p- A bridge with too much weight collapses.

P- Build another one using Pie?

p- Not literally. A building that does not bend breaks.

P- See Pie seeing past the bridge?

p- And building. And what we are building.

P- A happening?

p- Happening forward and up and up and up and to the top and over and over and over again and again. The mountain only seems so high. That is until you get to the other side.

It is fitting they are called faces.

P- Facing?

p- The sides of mountains- north, west, south, east. North face. East face. South face. West face. Always facing or faced.

P- This is Pie?

p- This is Pie.

P- Does this contradict the limited number of Pie?

p- Again with the numbers. Math, ok. Numbers, limiting. Yes, only a number. The beauty of the crumbs is the breakdown that occurs while reaching the end of Pie or rather the need for Pie by the time we get to the end of Pie and won't need crumbs either.

P- It will have served its purpose?

p- Ungreed.

P- It will have brought us there?

p- To the place of the unbought, unbroken, ungreedy soft edge of possibility.

P- Better get used to it?

p- Scarcity defines the very idea of excellence. If everyone is celebrated that must mean, we are endorsing mediocrity. There must always be losers built into their concept of success.

P- Bring more pillows (BMP). And the children?

p- It's a tough world out there. There will always be misery, better to make them used to it while they're small- a great wealth and power concept that there must always be winners and losers.

P- Social rebuke of giving trophies for participation?

p- A tantrum from the supposed adults in the room. Passing on of perceived and real pain and trauma. A system of abuse rooted in a moral conviction that you can't get anything, including love, appreciation, feeling good about yourself, unless you've earned it. In order to get into heaven you do not need more lectures and guilt trips about how capitalism will set you free. Same thing with great power and wealth, though conveniently omitting inherited and corrupted bailouts and handouts through said great power and wealth.

P- Hybrid of neoclassical economics and theology designed to drive us insane thinking everything is personal fault nefariously couched as personal responsibility. A hackneyed circle jerk?

p- Conditioning conditions that you are only good if you dot dot dot. This is not a bubble to break. Unless you count greed.

P- Riches equal expertise and status. What are the responsibilities of society to educate?

p- Distracted by how we make education more affordable. Education as commodity must end. Level the playing field. An educated populace contributes to the overall well-being of society. It strengthens democracy, participation, global health, and as a fundamental human right, makes us a better-rounded society.

Change the whole damn of the system. Those with great power and wealth have metastasized. End hierarchical access to knowledge.

Restructure systems of information. Don't add restrictions based on class. Private education is a bad idea.

My aren't you lucky you were born rich. No, I am a talented smart as fuck peacocker greased in oil and claimed ordained by above and deserving of everything I have. Good for me all the time feels.

P- What are our priorities? Budgets reflect our priorities. If we were to invest in education instead of instruments of violence and repression like prisons and endless war, imagine that society?

p- Inside self or outside self? Public vs. Private? Seen or unseen?

P- Who do these schools and universities serve?

p- Think of the journeys and stories yet to be lived, collected, and returned to the community. Actual great power and wealth.

P- But if you make education attainable to all, it cannot be stratified. The privilege veil will fall. Think of the mess. People learning about things that interest them. They might just grow and share and develop untold wisdom, power, and strength. And gifted, freely, uncoerced by profit, what would that do to society?

p- It would be awful and all kinds of tragic. I can't imagine the unchained imaginings that could go on.

P- But that's not the historical impulse behind education. Is it?

p- The democratization of knowledge? No. Those with great power and wealth might not feel so special and apart.

P- And that's why we are separated?

p- Public schools were never intended for everyone. As the riff raft was allowed in, the rich just came up with more ways to separate themselves from the peasants. The resultant achievement gap is not an unintended consequence.

P- The system is working?

p- Calling it broken is part of the busy business of trying to come up with a solution to a problem that is not a problem for those with great power and wealth. It is the solution. Which is why they will do everything they can to distract and divide us from so called fixing the so called problem.

No amount of tinkering is going to solve their desire to continue to exclude us from their halls of big greatness and prestige.

P- How do you struggle against a force that does not want you?

p- We throw an even better party and don't invite them.

P- Look?

p- We have to find some kind of intelligent way, to outsmart, out organize those who will out evil us, who will out bigot us. Listen. We're not going to play that game. We're not going to out bigot the bigots. We're not going to out evil the devils. That can't be what we do. That can't be the path that we go. But we can out smart them and we can out organize them. We have to start thinking really truly creatively.

Why did you not call it out when you have a voice louder and higher than ours?

P- I was too scared to lose what I thought I had. Am I weak?

p- Human. What does it say that it took Pie to calm the storm?

P- That it was never about one, for Pie is about the many. It is in the many, united, the energy force behind Pie drowning the lie of the individual as sacred. Defeating the lie that one cannot be an individual and still be a part of entirety. Lies told to us since money, resources, concepts of scarcity, became weapons against the threat of community. To empire, there must be not enough for all. A way to sell it to the masses, not enough to share, your worth is incomplete unless you compete. If you cannot or will not compete then you fail. You are a failure unworthy of nice things. You are a spot on their heel unworthy of nutritious food, warm shelter, good health and certainly not riches and abundance.

But there is always money for war and it's adventures. Not so fun.

In this they steal your time. For what is more precious than great power and wealth but time. Pie is time returned. Time slowed. Time lived. Time believed. Time not war. Pie is mindfulness of loving kindness now. So protected by many Pie believers, time personified, poised is the true peace of Pie. Units of Pie small, medium, and large are irrelevant. Each unit a vote for ungreed. One Pie or one crumb of Pie is still Pie. Kind of like being a little bit Pie. You are or are not. It is a gift of strength and power, great strength, and power regardless of size.

It is a failing of us to have seen, not seen. To now fight a lost cause. We did not act. We failed. We destroyed instead of created. We stifled intentions of the abled. We punished instead of loved. We harm because we are weak and inferior. Such so called greats were always going to fail and be replaced by the greater good of the many. Our inadequacies naked and on display embarrass us now. Now we are the worst of our imaginings. Now we are irrelevant. How do you make an exit when you have shit on your hands and face, frontside, and backside?

p- You slink away like the bad demon you are.

P- All great power and wealth is evil. All Pie, swirling around unstoppable, is here to cleanse. All crumbs deliver the taste of promised peace. It is our right. Those that say it is not, know less than a child. They spew taking and keeping as if stealing and hoarding will protect them from suffering. Such fools. They create the suffering and whine when faced with their own mortality.

I never meant to be bad and hurt anyone. I was wrong and I'm sorry. I want to change and do better. I want to be kinder. I want to be humble. I want forgiveness.

Can their intention be reformed?

p- The line between authority and plebeian is part of the construct of social contracts nobody but those in authority agreed to.

P- To not overwhelm. To underwhelm as enticement. Is that the aftertaste of Pie?

p- Most certainly. Pie, an imprint of and on world times to provide access that is not hyper adrenaline libertarian capitalism biased. To provide a frustratingly tearful touch. Never forgetting that as long as they steal from bodies like garden rabbit thieves in the night, it is fucking personal, you bet your fucking ass it is.

P- Is there rage?

p- Do I look mad?
Rage is being.
Only.
Pie.
Ungreed.

27

P- Can you buy your way out of a spiritual recession?

p- More like shop through regression.

Pie is a civic responsibility.

P- The adults have officially left the children to die?

p- Lame name the issues. A tabula rasa.

We are all deeply dissatisfied with the system. A capitalist system causing mass suffering and mass misery. But aren't we the best in the world? Most people don't even know how they're going to pay for their next meal. There are people making a lot by any global standard, that don't know how they're going to make ends meet. We have to restructure how humans coexist on this earth. Billions of humans under this monstrosity are barely able to exist or subsist.

P- Is Pie anti-capitalism, anti-imperialism?

p- Why yes, yes, it is.

A system where humans interact as bodies for profit is making life miserable on this planet. Is destroying life on this planet. Not Pie.

P- What is a better system of coexistence for humans overall?

p- Large systemic question or obvious moral question. The latter.

P- Good wealth or bad wealth?

p- Correct. Make it obsolete.

P- But how will people know what to strive for?

p- That is an asinine statement fed and put forth by corrupt asinine acolytes of great power and wealth. Don't be an idiot.

P- How will we measure success?

p- By everyone.

P- How will we keep resources scarce and all to ourselves?

p- You won't. You will share. Fatuous to think one individual can own air or water or earth. Idiots are no longer allowed questions.

P- How will I pretend to be better than everyone else?

p- You can pretend as you want but you won't need or want to.

P- How is this not a fantasy dream scape?

p- How else do you think we get there?

P- But even dreams are a limited resource. Part of the trick, eh?

p- Fuckers can't control us completely, yet.

P- The spectacle fools with images and slogans, norms and laws, only the meek pray to and obey?

p- I'm fully human, you are not. Yet, whatever they say sticks to me and does nothing to you. This is what must change.

P- Are those who cannot represent themselves going to be represented?

p- By hook or by crook. So many crooks.

P- We will need the cleverness of both, and interest from both sides of the brain. The left and the right.

Without a theory of revolution there can be no revolutionary movement? True or false?

p- True.

Revolutions require skilled organizers, self-discipline, an alternative ideological vision, revolutionary art and education.

They take fierce time and energy. They require commitment to the cause and unwavering commitment to cause change.

Revolutions are long, difficult projects that take years to make, slowly and often imperceptibly eating away at the foundations of power.

Successful revolutions of the past, along with their theorists, should be our guide, not the ephemeral images that entrance us on mass media.

P- It is said, fascism is big government run by corporations not the people. With overt and covert violence, a government animated by scapegoating, vengeance, and hate.

Their final objective towards which all their deceit is directed is to capture political power so that, using the power of the state and the power of the market simultaneously, they may keep the common worker in eternal subjection.

Using racism, faux nationalism, misogyny, homophobia, and the corruption of both democracy and the rule of law, fascists are cementing their power in state after state with extreme voter suppression, voter roll purges, gerrymandering, dismantling of checks-and-balances, and packing the courts.

About right?

p- People just want to be loved.
In the meantime-
fascism /făsh ĭzʹəm/
noun, not a hobby or a horse or an excuse to burn the house.

1. A system of government marked by centralization of authority under a dictator, a capitalist economy subject to stringent governmental controls, violent suppression of the opposition, and typically a policy of belligerent nationalism and racism.
2. A political philosophy or movement based on or advocating such a system of government.
3. Oppressive, dictatorial control.

So says The American Heritage® Dictionary of the English Language, 5th Edition.

P- And that's why they're so mean?

p- Enraged. They're simmering with white hot rage.

P- Like a pot about to boil?

p- Every accusation is a confession.

P- Is there another way?

p- Well, this way isn't working. So, yes.

P- Government is the problem?

p- The people running government are the problem and not really even the people but the so called chosen by the people running the government infected with the greed virus who are weak and stupid. Too stupid to realize how unsustainable their decisions are, too weak to stand up and have some self-control over the corrupting greed virus brought to us dear friends by the greed mafiosos called corporations, nothing cooperative about them unless you're a government contract looking for bailouts and a leg or arm or two or head up in handouts through lobbied for, legally bribed and bought favorable regulations. All the bribed. Are all evil.

P- You don't really believe they're all evil?

p- Greed is evil which is why it's a sin in every organized denominational affair. They confuse us with that strongest will survive and thrive shit, but we evolved out of and from that primal landscape. If we are to be the creative conscientious type, we profess to be. If we are to survive and not regress. If they expect to get away with this crime against the living and not end up deader than the thing they're already rotting in something like a demon cage, then new plans, new arrangements must be made.

P- This movement then?

p- There has to be a movement. There is a movement. You are enough. You are more than enough. You are not alone. You are part of the movement and will never be abandoned. Not by this power. This belief. It is already here. Has already percolated longer than a baby needs time to be a young adult. A happening, a movement, a revolution, language will work itself out. This one is just beginning. The people are deciding and deriding just in time.

You are not too late. You are not alone. You are just in time. You are just right in this moment. This is your moment. This is the moment. We love you. We see you. We need you. We are you.

P- If they can resist the greed virus?

p- Aw, fucker had to go and ruin the moment.

P- Unprecedented times call for unprecedented measures?

p- Yes really, yes so. Yes, on a grander larger scale than ever before. At no time have we been more connected. The stories that traveled miles and days, weeks, months, years, generations before, sometimes continents and centuries will and are available and shareable today. Watch the watchers though. Be careful.

It's the motives that are wrong and the easiest to change because they are free.

Motive 1- Not dominance
Motive 2- Not conquest
Motive 3- Not extraction

There is a lot more to our nature than posing stridently with sticks bigger than the last on top of an animal or hill and telling a story too small for nature's path. It is not our true path, but a hard turn overcome by right minded belief and being. A story of together not apart from. Powering not economies but holism through big babe steps of learning to walk and chew Pie at the same time.

P- And then we are not broken?

p- And then caring is enough. This is our responsibility. Out comes healing and joy as Pie is closer to us coming closer to it. For all Pie really is is a feeling and saying yes to mattering life and no to madder means of achieving solo sad life. That story is one of beauty and calm discovering harmonic palmy mystery for two.

P- Discomfort will bring strength. Part of being uncomfortable is knowing that it is working. The goal is improvement and growth. We cannot let the fear, shame, discomfort, and our desire to maximize comfort dictate our path alongside Pie because they say we will not grow. To become stronger makes one more capable. To become in shape, a shape of ourselves we see for ourselves, not long from now starts now through the balancing of evil and Pie.

We've never got it right, human beings. We are all a mess, and we're very early in our evolution. What is communal?

p- Cooperation is quintessential to our collective survival. We are more productive than we have ever been. Thriving will be the consequence of that when we let go of their tenuous griping grip.

P- The current system will cancel all prospects for a decent future?

p- You are not better than me, I am not better than you. A power system that distributes power amongst the people is not perfect but is aspirational in a way that does not make you blush in the morning. We can't put off a revolutionary confrontation with our torturous greed system much longer. The epidemiological, ecological, and nuclear clocks are close to midnight. The chance of building a Pie movement required to overthrow the extreme greed system is greater with our current democratic like system still intact than it is with overt fascism in power, of course it is. All fascism must be denied and resisted. In ways more aggressive and radical than anything our so called leaders are remotely willing to undertake, and in ways our so called leaders are strongly opposed. It must be denied and resisted in ways that set new terms for ungreed by demonstrating the awesome power of Pie amongst an aware and energized populace in public and private, and encourages all of us regular folk, the proletariat, to be liberated in a revolutionary Pie world and way of life beyond greed, despotism, libertarianism, imperialism, capitalism and all the greed systems that go along with capitalism's diseased reign.

P- Let's cancel the giant wealth generating machine with?

p- Permission
Validation
Acceptance
Support
Gentleness

Sorrow is the vitamin of growth. I feel like a teenager who stubbed a toe- I'm too old to cry but it hurts too much to laugh. Facing the painful process of renunciation leads also to emotional growth and maturity. Time to heal the trauma and end the cycle.

P- I am called a Pie Maker, a red and a radical. I admit to being all. I am what will end money obsession and replace it with a commitment to unity and others. Real or unreal?

p- Very real indeed as we plant the seed seeing blood for green and greed for our dead. Off with the ill hand as it comes for our head.
P- We, and our growing discontent, to put it mildly are a byproduct, an end result of the system they perpetuate against us. Who wants to play a game where only a few percent of a percent see any glory, with an even fewer taking the bulk of glory, and the vast majority getting no glory at all?

p- Pie Revolution is Collective Empowerment
(PRICE)

Community v. Collective.

eatm = to give/ leave an impression.

Minoritarian rule. Pie is majoritarian rule. Life is not a game.

P- If we've never seen times like this before, the solutions to the problems we face must be ones never seen before. The way out is going to look different than past solutions. We're going to have to create a dramatically new way of organizing ourselves. The breaking of patterns to form new ones. New ways of thinking, being, belonging to lands, and connecting to each other.

Adaption or extinction. Wildly utopian thoughts, organized around Pie, like sand running through an hourglass will bring us to a level of harmony not experienced and not properly explored without the misleading lure of profit prosperity.

Because the current trajectory is one of more madness. If those with great power and wealth haven't come for you yet, they will. No one is safe from the greed virus.

The more we adopt Pie, the more we become less dependent on their system and find relief and reliance together. Within those strong numbers we diminish their power. We stop the false misguided idolization of self, serfdom, and shopping.

The time crumbs of commodification and evil in the hourglass become Pie crumbs of supportive sustainability and sustenance.

The more we want Pie. The less needed it is. Not the more Pie we have but the more we think we need to have. Today's Pie suckers and evil eaters are not part of this new tribe. They are gone to the greed virus. It doesn't matter. Their Pie crumbs will flow to us soon enough. Without bloodshed or broken bones their debt is already being paid in the collective disgust, sadness, and rejection of wicked energy, now kind, flowing against and through them. Swept beneath their feet it blows back to us as filtered qi. Pulling us closer to Pie and further from maltreaters. No question.

28

P- The chaos serves a purpose. Sews the scene for a red caesar to save us. To suspend, in service of ending, democracy by an authoritarian mythological hero figure. Blowing everything up allows them the excuse to bring someone in to fix what they purposely broke to begin with. Not that things were working great, but the small semblance of guardrails was better than none. It increases libertarian and populist sentiment. Their vision is bold. The mess is the distraction and the point. Becoming an excuse to rearrange the chairs on the titanic ship of dreams being sunk. They do not want to completely destroy government. They want to continue to reshape it in total service of the rich and connected. How is that going to improve anybody's life but theirs?

p- It is fucking not. Aren't we too old to be told and gaslit too?

P- Nobody is coming to save you. As if that is not the feeling you've been having and resisting acknowledging all this time. There is no scarcity. They love a monster. Do you save yourself?

p- Or fall into the metal death hands of greed?

P- Or realize a rallying point found in Pie is about as gold as good gets?

p- It is quite flawed, the money part of it.

P- Or that is just the necessary modern trap of its outward trappings to lure in the common misguided greed sucker suckered by great greed not nature to find a way through, any way more, that gets eyeballs on and bodies through the door?

p- Don't you have a mouthful?

A doorway on a path beyond societies built on money and greed and competition-based rules, dictums and orders really. No way.

P- We're all fucked?

p- Yep.

P- Why is it always on the side of the oppressed to hold back, to be tempered, to follow a grievance etiquette?

p- We've been wrong all this time. Limited by greed in the name of tradition and the minority self-interest of those already with great power and wealth. Their myopic greed. The virus inside, spreads to those around them and influences downward. Their lack of compassion, their lack of interest in others, their lack of a different better wholly unimaginable, because they're too sick and simplistic in their greed-soaked ways, world, is what has held us back. Weak feeble minds and coal caked dry bodies lead us down a shaft. They stopped holding our lands long ago, we do it for them. We are all idiots back then.
These are not benevolent folks. These are monsters to be reviled and revolted by, not revered. The constant gaslighting causes us to lose our minds and our souls in the process. Shut up and sit down.

P- Embrace the alternative?

p- It is a matter of now and for the ages.

P- And what of this being, actually, the least interesting times we know?

p- That the moment we are living through can be characterized by one word?

P- And that word is?

p- I am coy.

P- Nothing complex about that?

p- Quite boring really.

P- But that these thought leaders were not so plain. And?

p- Boring. Whiny. Unoriginal. Weak boot licking blood feeders.

P- But are they not so great as they think?

p- Poor little babies. Helpless in their meaningless aspirations to be relevant.

P- What would you give them?

p- A binky.

P- What do they need?

p- A fucking spanking of great spiritual force.

P- Will that work?

p- Let's find out.

P- Instead of saying, oh how we chase the sun away, oh how we make the children pay, all because instead of bought, we ought not, and now night, and night, no knight are they to fight, so prey our Pie will save the day. True or false?

p- Let's talk about Pie.

P- And?

p- No and.

P- Is Pie just another greed system?

p- It is. I am still tired.

P- That a problem?

p- Yes.

P- How does that work?

p- After a wink. Where would your power be without your pain? Your wound?

P- Empathy?

p- Ditto disconnection. We are ending that system, remember?

P- Be careful, the sleep of reason, brings forth monsters. Are you familiar with borrowing from them as they have stolen from us?

p- I know this disease, the exaltation of race, religion and nation, the deification of the warrior, the martyr and violence, the celebration of victimhood. The cloaked believe they alone can control, through vice and virtue, (while we work and toil), cowardly and evil. They believe they alone have the right to revenge. Pain for pain. Blood for blood. Horror for horror. The familiarity is in the madness, like an old blanket, we keep it close.

P- Once these fires are lit, they cannot be stopped?

p- Which is why, at the outset of every war, we have to transform our enemy into the image of a demon, and then, since it is the devil we are fighting, we can hurt and kill others without asking ourselves all the spiritual questions that come with being at war and hurting other humans. We no longer have to face the realization that those we are killing are persons like us.

The killing and torture, the more they endure, contaminate the perpetrators and the society that condones their actions. They have ground us down until the capacity to feel is gone. Replaced by hate and death. They expand the moral injury of war. It is the complicity of an international community that licenses the malice of ethno-centric genocidal slaughter and accelerates a cycle of violence it may not be able to control.

The ones who see Pie the hardest often need falling hard the most.

P- We have broken the rules of nature. Pie is born. It is not a punishment. It is not a savior. It is a disruption to current systems. A course correction only if of sorts. A pause to the glitched flaw of leftover evils. A bit of bad has spoiled the porridge. Too much salt. Not even a squeeze of lemon works this time, over time.

This interruption to behavior, albeit wrought with similar symptoms of the disease. Greed and all. Pie. Begins to work in and on its seers like an anecdote. A holistic homeopathic balm to encourage root human bodily and spiritual systems to develop antibodies to the virus of greed. In turn our systems react uniquely yet uniformly to our already unique but uniform human selves.

Ah, against and not with is the source problem addled and ailed. Ungreed through a sustained shared approach. Quite logical and sensible. Success of self and feeding of source Pie is more mutually assured. Pie in tandem in a selfless method. Is more.

For some there is a natural calm loving kindness to us and our kin. This is the thing we do to take care of ourselves and our kin to insure against the future.

For others, time is the price paid as the seemingly heightened level of profit accrues instead in titular chaos. A perceived frenzy. A drug like rush of varying effects. High, low, excitement, panic. An urgency for more. The animal runs into doorways and walls trying to consume the uncomfortable need very much like greed.

Aha, it is during moments of greed induced haze, ecstasy, and dis ease that the healing crisis manifests itself. Learned and bumping against us, rough edged or less so, we can feel torn apart or merely yoked about. This is Pie working on you.

With curved degrees around and in between, Pie works on you in unsuspecting ways. It is math doing its math. There is no you figuring it out. That is the trick it plays and eventually everyone must go through. Don't criticize or congratulate yourself with way in and way out genius moves. Stand still instead. You think you are an active participant but that is an illusion. This deceptive destruction is necessary to ween us off the myth of self. Life is not standing still but sometimes with Pie the best move is none.

We have promulgated the myth of self over community so long we are not to be trusted with getting to peace and compassion without an analytical non-hypocritical intervention to push us out of the den of individual yet collective consumer delusion and despair. Do you see how needs of self and greed begin to melt away?

p- That it is as seers of Pie we empty the helpless emptiness of self in exchange for fullness in cooperation with others as we build community one seer at a time.

P- While?

p- Whilst math maths.

P- While?

p- Whilst Pie Pies.

P- Through?

p- To.

P- Up, and over, and beside?

p- Yes.

P- What do we tell the ones who see Pie the hardest?

p- They may fall hardest.

P- And those that see Pie the softest?

p- You have the least hard to fall.

P- Does it sound a theorem?

p- It doesn't matter to math. The math rings. As time.

29

P- Do we have major problems as a society?

p- Yes, we do.

P- Are those with great power and wealth going to figure out any solutions to our problems?
p- Of course not. It is against their interests to do so. Their endless grievance fest is exhausting. Every human being is inherently built to benefit mankind, the pursuit of wealth is not. It is guided by a benefit of, for, and to one. Monopolies are anti us.

P- Is this a tragedy or comedy?

p- Like all epic tales, it is a tragedy of proportion and a comedy of redundancy.

P- Government could be an extension of family. A large community whereby, like in a family, people assume different roles, a properly motivated, with limited intentions, governing body of people is no more controversial or distrusted then who takes out the garbage or whether we have cake or pie for the next holiday gathering.

The greed virus has influenced current forms of governance to be controlled by corrupt people with malformed intelligence and malignant morals. A vacuum has sunken the sun. A crater really. Pie, with it being formed on an unspoiled unspoken level of trust unknown to humans, is a logical, necessary, primary step in achieving good on a promise of fairness and accountability.

Now however, they'll say you want them to join your cult. They already have, haven't they?

p- Their perverted religion of selfish profit is based on human suffrage. Wasted corpses laid bare so they can profit blood from our tree of life a little more.

Our belief is sourced from compassion and guiltless righteousness. The sacral knowledge that we have must be shared and passed amongst us. It is a sacred duty to do more than just bear witness to the monstrous inhuman treatment of our fellow travelers in this world.

P- Do the tired and downtrodden not get a pause to tend to their own wounds?

p- Of course they do. It is for those that cannot fight, those that do not have autonomy that we band together to correct the sins of the greedy. As there is no trust in those that have great power and wealth, we come together to fuel Pie. Pie is a steppingstone of collective consciousness, one block of numbers at a time building a stream to become a river of movement and energy.

P- We have a duty to the planet, it's species, and ourselves?

p- They would have us look away. Give up. Say it is too hard. There is too much to tackle. Why bother but the fish still jump.

P- Because you are only one person?

p- But we're not. Pie is an example of the unifying force that shifts entire planes of being and understanding. Random, anonymous, caring individuals coming together for a variety of motivating factors.

P- This is the big one?

p- This is the one that tops them all and topples what they want us to succumb to, inscrutable, insurmountable markings of greed.

P- This is the one?

p- If greed is the problem, Pie is the solution. There is nothing more important than fixing our gaze, one pair of eyes at a time, and righting that which destroys. Greed is evil. There can be no peace as long as they run evil roughshod through our souls. There is no practical or moral equivalence. No more gaslighting to be had. We see them and they see us for the threat to their power that we are. You are not alone. None of us will mock or use fear to drive you into the safety and future of Pie. You are seen. You are heard. You are cared for. You are believed. You are not alone. You are a part of this big, bold, beautiful beast of reason and possibility. For time, but not yesterday.

P- What other choice is there?

p- None. Choice is an illusion.

Artists imagine that another world is possible. Pie is art. It is the creative expression of distaste and distrust in our current greed system. Checked shamed greed can die. Expressions of art, beauty, compassion live forever. It's as simple as saying no to ongoing war and suffering and yes to prosperity and kindness.

P- And the greed narrative will crumble?

p- Together, one infection at a time.

P- Tasteless opulence is not the cure to a fever?

p- Pie makes power uncomfortable. It says- we don't need your stinking system anymore. We don't want you running things anymore. You did it wrong so we're going to fix it. Let's go. You can't play us for rubes anymore.

P- They will do everything to control pie. To take it away from you.

It is your obligation to make power uncomfortable. That is what makes one's duty as a citizen admirable. Feebleness will slow. We are the root culture we crave. Do our work and power protection rackets will scatter like mice?

p- After, egocentric victimhood. They are the biggest babies. When you have been beaten, to beat back is sound earned logic. Our fists are not wrapped in blood cloaked esteem. They will do this and more. We demean them and bring them dishonor.

We define the value of Pie using kindergarten esoterics. Like, the primary cancer in society is money in politics. Like, many of the deadliest cancers are preventable. No more secret or public wars.

P- Pie cures cancer?

p- Don't be daft. We cure cancer. Pie is just a tool to help us along the way. It is not a solution to greed or the traumas that cause greed. Pie is a mechanism. An aid. Nobody is coming to help us. You, me. It's not the same as being alone, doing it all on our own. Having ever smaller finite tribes of so called like-minded persons whom we trust and therefore want to protect and care for. Pie teaches us that greed is limited but a greater whole is stronger and more powerful than its parts. We are part of a whole whether we isolate or not. We are connected whether we think we are or not. Pie shows us that tricks and sabotage to our internal and external selves and world only weaken us.

P- They like that part, us weak. Disunity hides their symptoms?

p- For the evidence is in the symptoms of the virus greed. We think others ill and ill informed. We are all ill and in need of reform. Pie is simply an accounting tool to show us all how to be accountable to each other again and for good. We've had such moments in private and in the pockets of time immemorial. Those with great power and wealth have whittled away our shields.

Let Pie be armor against such evil destructive forces. It will not judge you.

Know the double speak serves one purpose- to speak for you.

P- And if nothing changes? Do we see where we're headed?

p- We're all going to die. It's not off a cliff. That demise is too merciful for the illness of greed. Know, and never forget, the path of greed is not hyperbolic. Headfirst. Eyes open. Hearts closed. The end is face down this side of the mountain, dark and lonely.
P- And so we begin?

p- The journey has already been too long, too unkind, too cruel.

30

P- That's the big lie they want you to believe, that you have no real power. That you have no ability or means to reach thousands or millions of people. You do. You hold it right now in your hands. It is never going to end unless you stop them. Take money, power, and influence out of their hands.

How is trust established after centuries of greed, theft, and disappointment?

p- Through humbly crumbly moments with Pie.

Trust yourself, trust Pie. Pie is us. Pie my oh my. Yum Pie.

P- Is there choice or adherence to the idolatry of greed?

p- This is not hard. Choose not the slow death of greed but the instant unexploited life of Pie. Not a choice, choice is like alternative facts or anything you disagree with being not news.

P- Stop conforming. Stop doing what they tell you to do. You can feel it isn't right. That's because it's not. They try to scare you off and away from the thing that makes them extinct. That is how they survive and thrive at your expense. When you take a different path the landscape changes and the horizon is both a greeting and an end to their violence. Encountered head on, unabashed, unafraid, you do and become the thing they fear most. Independent of their garbage violent system of greed. Pie releases you from that evil. There is no longer guilt associated with actions to pacify your growing sense of unease and mistrust of the rot. Pie is pure math. There are no hidden corners for secrets, greed, and mold to grow and fester. How are you doing with all this?

p- I have moments of doubt it may not be happening.

P- Me too. There are few if any behaviors or activities that you have to know everything about in order to participate or do them. Participation is the key point. We make manifest a destiny determined by us. Not them. Their great power and wealth are no match for our great power which will beget a wealth not limited by things. Only things. Versus a sense of time and place and calm comprised of nonviolence and beauty.

They've bought you. Cheap. But you are no longer for sale. Plundering your labor and soul, your value reduced. Pie is a return of time. Your precious energy is returned. Pillaring strength and health. A different kind of wealth. Trust yourself, you know?

p- It's all too much. None of what's been done to try to change our trajectory from mass greed has worked. Instead, the narratives against compassion and unity only grow. As can be seen in the same fear-based narratives around Pie.

P- Ultimately, that is the signal to follow. If they are afraid, then it is a worthwhile endeavor to engage with, no?

p- Ultimately, greed is about control.
We aim to make sense of the uncontrollable.
When we feel out of control, we hold on even tighter.
With all their great power and wealth they are still small inside.
In their deepest parts is a shallow grave.
Hoarding immense means is their way of feeling in control.
It is wrong.
It is the wrong approach to feeling safe and connected.
It is mean.
They are not happy.
They are mean.

Not confident or comfortable.
Desperate.
That is why they lash out.
That is why their greed is never ending.
That is why we feel the disruption of a human connectedness.
Their misery is our misery.
That is how the virus spreads.

P- We are all going to die. Are we back to that?

p- It is a late-stage empire proverb.

P- It's our intro to an out. Pie is a breathing dichotomy to be sure.
It is, and it isn't cheap.
It's slow and it's fast.
It's public and it's private.
It is money but it is not.
It takes time, it saves time.
It is just math, but also just people.

And more?

p- We've been on the wrong course for hundreds if not thousands of years. It feels too hard. We feel too tired. Too vulnerable. It is hard to trust anything, anyone, anymore.

P- That's why it's a good thing we are not dealing with bullshit methods of the past like plain old boring greed. If we are going to welcome and build a future worth living, then we need to actually act like that's where all of this is heading and take the steps that will get us there. Pie is that step. One fucking step at a time or it's over. None of us get anywhere though if greed is our motivation.

Are we building a sort of new romanticism?

p- Crepuscular and ancient dross?

P- What about them?

p- We'll get to use words and phrasing like that, and they won't be considered pretentious.

P- Really?

p- Ok, maybe not but it was worth a try.

P- Has a new war begun?

p- An old war is about to end.

P- Are we still all gonna die?

p- Maybe.
It's not ok.
Nobody's coming to save us.
It's not ok.
And for what?
It's not ok.
A call to fingers and toes.

P- Ok, we are not there yet so language still matters. Reality matters. No matter what they say or how they warp it, right?

p- Got it. The amusement phase has passed. The intelligentsia, artists, poets, thinkers, tech head wizards and prophets of our day are worn down by the very tools they rely on to express themselves. It seems there is nothing original anymore, though that conversation has been had more than once before. Though music, the notes are old and more. None is a substitute to the smoke-filled coffee house of old. This is where we continue to reference the past, borrow not beg from it, and incorporate history as learning that leans towards the future we are building.

P- We stop elevating the individual?

p- Yes. But, for now though, rapacious technology still has a mass buy-in. Handheld technology is ubiquitous and hegemonic. We surrender our privacy, agency, and power by relying on them too much. This is an obstacle. The rulers and owners of this tech are the infected. They are taking as we think we are making. More content is not the answer. Without action it is a distraction.

P- It's not about individual entities, the system is shattering. All those representing and functioning under the system espouse and uphold hollow rhetoric and policies.

Those with great power and wealth, live in a glass house at the top of a pyramid. And?

p- They think themselves kings, queens, princes, and princesses.

P- They serve on the surface on which an image is painted. And?

p- But this painting is painted by the system.

P- Greed nation doesn't love anybody. It's an empire in decline folding in on itself. Disposing of any one or thing not in allegiance to their system. The virus needs to spread. If it begins to eat itself, it will not thrive. It will die a death constricting all obstacles in its path. Not like a small mammal in quiet inevitable retreat of life. This empire screams to hide its anger at losing. Blaming everything around it instead of seeing it was hubris that took it down. Greed forever is unsustainable. Greed is stoppable.

It's just a matter of will. And?

p- Will there be anything left after the virus's rage runs through it?

P- We're an unconscious civilization. When do we all get disenchanted enough to change the narrative?

p- Empires fade when they run out of impetus. Snippets tell tales.

P- What happens if Pie isn't distributed to everyone?

p- By then it won't matter.
In short time too long to tell.

We'll have come to take the whole damn Pie.

P- What does that look like?

p- It's either willful ignorance, insanity, or evil incarnate of them to think they can keep it all to themselves. Pie is us, not those with great power and wealth. They lumber at the mercy of greed. We glide with the blessing of ungreed. The moment, that moment, when that is finally reached, when actual human potential begins in earnest alignment with true beauty will be beautiful.

Just that. Beauty be.

P- We're all going to die on the current trajectory. What do we do? What do we do?

p- What choice do we have?

P- What choice do we have?

p- Lucky us. Not a choice. Oh, it sounds so terrible. Written in stone. They've won. They've won. Give up now. It's almost funny if it wasn't so sad. But it is already done. We have accepted Pie. Enough of us have already led the way. No need to worry about the initial heavy lift or fret about the little things. The news is good with Pie. We inspire each other by doing good, obviously.

P- The front-line Pie news is good?

p- Totally. Pie is meaning. Pie is no harm. Pie is good sensation. The opposite of our current incarceration. We are good corrupted. Ground down by abuse. Overused by long white death fingers picking our pockets and teaching us to hate no pocketed others. Every moment Pie succeeds, the red hand of the abuser slips a little bit more. Their grip is not as tight. But still not slight. Part of this has to do with their messiah complex. They just can't fathom that we can find strength in each other and not them. Rallying around Pie is the opposite of being corralled by them. They loathe our belief in meaning and purpose. They hate us because we have not fallen to our knees. They refuse to see our faces in each and every crumb of Pie because they are dead and ugly inside. They are not leaders. They are uninspired monsters.

P- Isn't that always the way with a bully?

p- A big slab of Pie slapping them in the face might quiet them for a while but wait till they get a load of us learning the recipe to Pie where we never go hungry or powerless or unsafe again. The abuser can't hurt us anymore. Bullies are so boring. All this unreal time spent on heartless incuriosity. Not so economical.

P- And all the time and sweat filled moments spent thinking and praying for them to just love you enough to stop. To see you as a soul carrying being worthy of kindness and respect just becomes grist of the past once Pie is embraced. Effort goes poof?

p- There is no more past or present praying for the pain to stop. Resiliency is our currency. Pie is the light that kills the darkness. Poof or pop there goes the evil weasel into its corner.

P- Will greed's evil hibernate only to come back again stronger?

p- Nope. It is so boring now. They want to kill everything fun. They destroy everything they touch. The juiceless is dry gone cry.

P- What happens to the greed memory?

p- We keep it as a talisman, a relic to collect dust ever so slightly seen out of the corners of eyes to remind us of where we've been, until eventually, the evil is just another faceless boogeyman in a long-gone world. A bedtime story to amuse the young.

P- Greed trauma salved by Pie as salvo for tomorrow?

p- As we carry on with our daily works it fits neatly next to us. In front of us, we push this beauty in whatever way is fitting for us. Through acts of creativity and compassion. We are the new care takers, and we want our home to be as beautiful on the inside as it is becoming on the outside.

P- A renovation of the soul?

p- We suffer from a collective failure of imagination that results from an intentional attack on our ability to process information. The resulting discombobulation, overwhelm, and trauma hurt us in physical ways by causing stress on the body; in mental ways by causing stress on your brain; and in spiritual ways by causing stress on our very being.

Therefore, a rebuilding of the soul after centuries of war is in order. Don't be fooled. There are many battles yet to come. We must prepare our thought arsenal wisely to not deplete so quickly.

P- And when we are tired and weak? Or scared it is not real?

p- Rest and recover. The trauma of centuries of abuse is heavy with evil's sticky dripping complaints. For it is always your fault things are not better. It is always you that is the problem. It is always some bad choice you made along the way to deserve this miserable fate.

P- And if we become impatient and angry?

p- Of course you will. Of course, we are. But do not let yourself become an abuser if you think it a shortcut to safety or relief.

P- What if you're despondent from the mass murder and violence?
p- Of course you are. You're expected to just shrug it off as it hollows your heart and neuters your mind and body, slowly then quickly. Don't let the bastards get you down when you're already low. As sure as they are bastards, they will continue to kick you when you are down. We must get back to the work of Pie works.

Like a gospel. Like a cathedral filled with singing open hearts. Or our birthday. Our new, very real birth day to celebrate not being an automaton but a fleshy gooey Pie giving and receiving human.

So, if you are still scared or sad that is a good thing. It means you still have a heart, and they haven't eaten your soul. You are healing this hole inside you as Pie heals the gaping rotting evil infested wounds of our world. A little bit of Pie goes far. As far as we're going together.

P- It is liberation?

p- It is.

P- What do we do during the in between moments?

p- Don't let the assholes get you down. You're going to need your strength. Eat some pie, before we eat them.

P- How do we accept the greed in the Pie community?

p- Another residue. It won't last. It will take some time, but they won't need or want that more more much where we're going.

Once you see our new land, you can't unsee it. It's not falling down the hole per se, more like falling up. Unlike the failing upward that so much greed invites to those with great power and wealth.

It will be a pressure and a release that moves such concentrations of Pie. They will guard it fierce. Defend its use, purpose, their right, they earned it, on and on the excuses they will whine. The more tears that fall the closer we know they are to the crack of surrender.

P- They'll just give up the greed?

p- Greed will give up on them. It is a tool and a virus; it needs use and food. It will be starved of attention and simultaneously ostracized from the crowd. Little becomes big as big becomes too bored and ashamed of a greedy life alone.

P- As if to be a child again. What the masses want has never been a priority before. What the masses need has never been a priority for them. The old and current ways only help a few while silencing the many. Except they've used, very effectively, distractions to encourage all the loud-mouthed yelling. Is this the bully bribing us with a fake idol bullhorn to trick us into believing we have a voice and therefore power?

p- Remember, they want to kill imagination while duping us into believing it was our idea to start. This is going to be the opposite of anything conceived in the past. It already is. Future us. Pie as energy has no time and place. It follows the will of us. That mass, teaches and informs us. An undercurrent taking place with so much force we feel it above us.

P- A ceiling to strive to?

p- Ceilings are for the incurious like them. Which is why they'll never be satisfied. Never be stopped on their own. Like fish in a fish tank, round and round orange greed ass biting green greed ass.

That ceiling is what Pie has already broken through. Like an atmospheric layer we have moved the mark. The mark is no longer us.

P- Why isn't it happening faster?

p- An appeal to logic in a land of sadness, rage, assholes, and disillusionment requires a matching of sensation. Thirst must be met with water. Those without shelter must have a home. A hungry child must have nourishment. This is the smoothing of edges. We must imagine a color that does not exist, yet.

P- Pie has already grown so much, but it is still childlike?

p- It's essence came upon us fully formed. Yet, like children, fits and starts and growing smarts is how a garden grows. Early still, it is not too late. We are just in time.

P- Pie is a leap of faith like another form of value. That old form is limited. Not by a structure like Pie but by the lack of imagination when greed is in play. In the greed repository the virus only wants to survive. It is only thinking about itself. How incurious and boring a story. This is a systems problem.

Pie then, becomes the voice to be heard rattling the cage of great wealth and power. If the ungreedy voice mattered, was heard enough to effect change, we would not have a need for Pie. A combination of self-regulation and system regulation. It doesn't much matter now because the system has already failed the many.

Pie as a system is by and for the many. Hence, no need to break, break down, break into it in order to effect change. The smallest crumb of Pie is change, is a voice finding the light.

Everybody needs to answer for more than just themselves. Idolatry of self is not only lonely but leads to the destruction of others. In turn, the very self you've sought to protect and vainly comfort is hurt. The circular logic is a fallacy. Their great power and wealth, our desperate attempt to belong, to keep up, is ruin.

Pie does not appear easy to some. Or it appears too easy to others. How does one make the approach without pain or hypocrisy?

p- Silent is different than quiet. Pie is stealth. It is dexterity. There are multiple entry points and exits if one finds themselves in too fast, too hard, too much, too soon. Quiet and calm and without urgency is an appropriate approach. Though unlikely once Pie is fully grasped.

Join Pie to start. The current system is not zero sum, but Pie is. If what they are doing makes you mad and sad then being Pie solvent makes them less solvent.

Remember, these are monsters trying to own it all, including you. The moment requires sustained outrage. We just keep going because the alternative, that this nightmare becomes tolerable, that the monsters infect and destroy this beautiful planet, means we've conceded. That is simply not an option. Not on our watch.

P- They want to hurt the people they hate. They want to ground them into dust and laugh while they do it.

The traumatized continue the cycle. Hurting those that they perceive hurt them. Since they can't burn their victimizer, they burn those they can. Why can't we all just get along?

p- Democracy is just a fancy word for everyone working, doing, and living together. Greed is war is death is death for democracy.

A new system for establishing value vs. growth. For growth to continue the insatiable must also grow. It should never feel better to buy a bigger yacht than build houses or feed hungry people. Let alone, enact policy through economic coercion, to create the instability that results in displacement and hunger. Spiritual displacement and hunger are also whose roots go back to the greed of others. If you are constantly working to feed corporate growth and just get by, you have no time or energy left to find a home, make a home, and feed your soul. Inspiration, creativity all wither in an environment or merely surviving.

P- It is not your fault you were not born into great wealth and power, and it is not your fault you are not able to achieve past the propagandist dream fiction that we live in a meritocracy. We do not. There are people that through hard work yes and a lot of luck achieve greatness of a specialized sort. Yet, not everyone is destined to be great at a physical or artistic profession. Those that are referred to here are not the magnificent in various fields. The ones who ruin it all are in the business of selling and destroying human capital in the name of capital.

Nowhere in the current system is there room for ordinary people. Those no less deserving of comfort and dignity. For there is no one actually worth billions more than anyone else in terms of their actual value to this planet. No how nowhere does that equation make sense. Does it?

p- These destroyers. These monsters. These psychopaths and sociopaths are no longer to be trusted with anything anymore. Their great power and wealth must be neutralized. They must be silenced and shamed. They do not even try to be magnanimous or appear as great benefactors of society and culture through building museums, parks, places of wonder and beauty. Instead, they create fat charities run by fat fingered so thought respectable mobster monsters. It is a transparent attempt at do goading and nothing like do gooding. Foundations built on a foundation of rot, privilege, and trickle down to themselves schemes. All completely legal and sanctioned by this corrupt system. Not broken. Working just as planned and running smoothly to keep the cracks of their disease protected by some tax write offs here, there, wherever the complicit lawyers find or write them. This playing by the rules oh but you wrote the rules is nothing to brag about or be proud of.

Not to be trusted. Not to be liked or admired. Pie got going among the masses and will continue to be supported by the masses, lest they get their greedy wench arms around its potential. Now they try and have in a number of ways but those are not ways too suffocating at this point to strangle and defeat the nature of Pie.

P- You either believe in equality, dignity, and safety for all, or you don't. It is crucial to be decent and have appropriate responses when faced with indecency. This is what it means to be human. To respond in kind to their way will only make you into a monster too. The greed virus is quite contagious, best not to get close to those infected. Will their smart money mindset prevail?

p- There is no such thing as smart money. Those with great power and wealth are not smarter or better, they are certainly not gooder, than anyone else. If they were, the evidence would be all around us that their system works. No, we do not need more or a purer form of their system to see what could be. If only they had their way more is not an answer and most certainly is not a solution. They are the problem. What they are infected with is the problem.

There is no actual, let alone good, reason we can't have and be at peace together. All with safe dry shelter together. Hot and nourishing food in our belly is not out of reach, it is intentionally kept from us. The trauma perpetrated upon us is not our fault. It is not a consequence of our choices. It is a symptom of the disease they will never seek treatment for.

We are the ones to end the virus of greed. A piece of Pie is our awaited medicine.

P- Is your value system in the way of accepting things as there are?

p- Yes. I require big good works to end this big bad mess.

P- How dare you?

p- Is this the best we can do?

P- Where does Pie go?

p- Into every crevice we put it.

P- Where is the connective thread?

p- Us. We found this amazing thing, each in our own ways, each with our own motivations for accepting and understanding it. Using it. Proselytizing about it in our own ways. Or staying silent about it for fear of derision or ridicule.

It found its way inside of us, through us, all around us. Informing us in ways never expected or imagined. Over time though we have seen it explain things, behaviors, and thoughts inside of us. We can explain it better ourselves, too. This, over time, is its special power. To change us. Slowly, quickly, we become the change that is Pie.

P- Will the response be appropriate?

p- We mustn't become the thing we are escaping. Victim must not become perpetrator. Greed must not turn into internal and external oppression.

We found our way to Pie by seeing an outsized need for a different system. The current system is not lacking. It is not broken. It was designed, implemented, and continues to be executed in precision predictable fashion. We see and breathe and feel in our bones and guts its limitations.

P- Is this really the best we can do?

p- Where is the imagination?

P- It's on a ticker. Doesn't that make it the same as the old?

p- It makes it the same as anything beautiful, precious, and unique. Anything ours to nurture and grow. Anything mine and yours.

P- But they're trying to strangle it?

p- The infection is here. The fever grows. We won't choke.

P- But the greed, seeping in too much, is it too much to do?

p- Priorities askew.

P- Big works?

p- A Pie works action, in thought and deed.

P- To solve for?

p- Any and all big issues and ideas.

P- Too big?

p- Only as big as our imagination.

P- What does the world begin to look like?

p- There is a need to turn you into something that you are not. To make you small and inconsequential. To keep you believing there is change just around the bend if only. These lies are transparent. There is no hope any old way is going to achieve any new result. Lulled and overstimulated by their distractions the grind ticks on. The grift has nothing standing in the way of ever more profit for the sick minded greedy few. The banality of evil is complete.

Let their loser loud mouthed puppets and pets complain and cry and whine. They point shiny fingers and pretend it is a light worth seeing. They breed headaches and hurt bellies from all their incessant whining. Maybe we are supposed to build statues to them and bow down before the cold metal reliquary of useless idolatry to make them feel better about kicking the shit out of everything sane and beautiful. They beg for violence as an excuse to ratchet up the inhumanity used against us.

But I am still hungry. You are still without warmth. Babies are not without pain wherever. Blood billy clubs of those with great power and wealth are a red sticky indictment of their soullessness.

It's not about how much you have or about getting more. It's the message it sends. Pie kicks them in the balls for a wider net for us.

P- Do they all end up dead?

p- They are already. Still biting us on the way down dead empire.

We are reimagining our societal structures. Consequences for those that infect with greed in perpetuity. Pie is the thread to strip them of what holds this nightmare together. To rid us of this plague, Pie served up, individually and collectively, binds us together while weakening them. Pie is a vote against thousands of years of wrong thinking and wrongdoing. Pie is what binds us against them, from the bottom up. Concentration of great power and wealth has already been tried and shown to benefit no one other than those with great power and wealth. It is an absurd lie and myth that somebody owning more of everything is going to somehow make your life better, magically. That sort of evil magical thinking doesn't make any sense because it is nonsense. It is also scary and very dangerous because we are living in systems that rely on that lie to keep everybody below from rising up.

Exceptions to the rule only prove the rule is already firmly in place and only a few are ever allowed to cross into their echelon. Systems need rebuilding not destroying. Institutions need to be separated from the untoward influence of biased moneys. People we choose to speak for us must be made to heel before us not those that would and handily bribe them through all too legal means. Accountability starts and ends with us. Humans are a cooperative species. We need, like, and love each other as a means of survival and for the ever more elusive state of thriving. Tearing it all down does not end the greed that got us to where we are. It actually makes it harder for those rotten souls responsible for this mess to ever have to answer for the mess they made.

There was a brief period of time where those with great power and wealth were not so awful. They looked out for their workers and gave back to the communities where they set up businesses. They may not have needed to look out for their neighbors, others with great power and wealth, but they invested in the areas they lived and elsewhere as a means of giving back. We've come to a point where they can no longer be trusted to safeguard, look out for, let alone better anyone but themselves and those with similarly vested interests. They blow it over and over again like a sad sad whore.

This moment was not arrived at without others aiding them along the way hoping to curry good favor and rise to their level of great power and wealth. And influence. That is what power and wealth do. Separately, but especially together, these poisonous attributes influence in all the wrong ways. No longer do the masses have any say over these systems. No longer are there safe reliable means of talking back, let alone taking back what those with great power and wealth hoard for themselves. The selfishness is a terminal disease.

33

P- Should we build monuments in their honor?

p- When they are gone, we will have a grand celebration lasting many days. Bullies and losers should only be remembered as reminders. They do not need rewarding for selfish bad behavior. Even though they are sick with the greed virus, treatment requires diligence and complete intolerance of their infectious treatment of those without great power and wealth. Societies will never be healthy so long as they are allowed to flit about spreading disease.

P- Pie will let those without great power and wealth change our trajectory?

p- Pie possesses the core values of what it means to be human. It pops the pustule of greed and shame. It gives aim and breadth to the human condition. It removes, slowly then suddenly, the obstacles that have been in humanity's way since all time became a commodity all the time.

P- It saves time?

p- It rescues time from sacrifice.

P- It is strong enough to support grand gestures?

p - It is as strong as we have been distracted and deceived.

P- What does all their great power and wealth bring?

p- Exactly. Once you know about Pie, it is obligatory to do something with this new profound knowledge. It is not enough to just stand by while great evil persists. It is not enough to just look after your own Pie. We are in this mess because we have not done enough to stop those with great power and wealth before this bunny fucking replicating mentality infected society. You don't correct for a problem by becoming part of the problem. You don't take Pie for granted and you don't let this opportunity, to create such real change we never knew is possible, get pissed on and away by the sick evil do badders that brought society to this avoidable reprehensible mess. Ugh, these assholes are exhausting.

P- They have money. Access to money. Access to those in related industry. Ability to network. So why aren't they doing more?

p- We are told progress is slow but assured. That is just the way things are. That future is possible because we say so. They need bigger pockets to hold their pockets. They are not real leaders.

P- The irony of Pie is that it is very fast patience. Funny and huh?

p- We need to help the overwhelm/ overwhelmed. And those fraught looking around them and knowing that it doesn't have to be this way. We lead ourselves because they dropped all balls.

P- Interlocking agendas are determined to destroy greed nation's government, as we currently know it, to weaponize the means of power and profit while also creating the perfect situation to coup again the government- to transform it into a permanent fascist regime. No one will for sure save us then. It is happening here.

Those with great power and wealth are hostile to the work we must do. We must go above and around them. Never down, for those with the least power and wealth are never ever to blame for the failures we encounter. The intentional pitting of us against each other and those with the smallest voice is only a tactic to be aware of and not succumb to.

Little efforts and actions are worth it because they help us practice and rejuvenate. Can you think of a color you have never seen?

p- I see it.
Relaxing and nourishing ourselves.
Finding a flow state, where our qi is moving smoothy.
Being calm, clear minded, and present.

P- People can only take great power and wealth at the expense of others. They pretend it is others that keep us down. Are they the true other?

p- A mental illness infects them to the ill effect we all suffer daily.

A system of living based on the procurement and consumption of capital is a symptom of an incurious life. This word is not real, just as money is not real. Just as money is not Pie and Pie is not money, Pie is very real and a symptom of a healing crisis currently underway.

P- Pie is a value system. The current system is one of procurement and consumption. Very complicated and very simple. So complicated it becomes a blur and you can see through to the singular point of it all. You take what they want, not for you but to cut their fever. To additionally slow the spread of the greed virus, you strike back at their means of production. The virus can't mutate and grow if you starve it. That is how we grow our Pie?

p- We have more power and wealth than we will ever know. It is precisely that detail they desperately don't want us to figure out.

P- Name some evils ruining humanity?

p- Misogyny, racism, poverty, & war.

P- That's four. Four gaslights lighting the common square?

p- Right, I grieve now of them tearing us to shreds. There's more than four, many much more more of toxic authority that is part of the more more machine.

P- That would be the tiered structure of our stratified economy which drives poverty and equals a new colonialism where countries, corporations, and militant groups extract resources and labor. Our resources and labor, at what cost?

p- Sick greed fuckers never stop with the pop pop of murder.

These cry babies are utterly hysterical lest it be suggested that those without great power and wealth might need a leg or hand up from time to time. Never mind that helping out your neighbor next door, down the way, or way far across the way has direct and indirect benefits to us all. Least of all being it is the least shitty way of going about being an uninfected greed fucked human.

P- They sound and look like screaming banshees one should normally just ignore. Yet here we are. You are just a foot soldier to them. Surrender, die more. Just another dolt bolt in the system, facilitating the machine whirring on and on with no interruption.

Pie is interference in the machine. Pie, at any price, says no, and yes, and I matter, just as much as you.

Pie, at its heart, is a vote saying no to yesterday, yes to tomorrow, and that we all matter in this moment.

These are not credible people. Not serious people. You must not ever rely on them to make the change. How could you?

p- Of course we can't. Whoever has the power decides where resources go. Whoever has the power controls resources that benefit all of us.

P- Revolting monsters. Try not to throw up thinking about them. You'll need sustenance and energy to eradicate the disease they embody.

This is a collective sickness. Even those of us who think they have won. Those of us who keep our head low and just try to carry on. Those of us who pretend nothing's wrong. All of us. We are all sick with the byproduct of millennia of greed.

Do you have the suspicion that one is being openly murdered? A drip drip of poison in your veins each time someone with great power or wealth, or one of their venal viral spreading accomplices, tells you not to believe the hunger, thirst, cold, overwhelm, and pain you see and feel?

p- Why yes. Their acquisitive nature is a lack of nurture from society as a whole. Let's fillet their salacious unequinimity.

34

P- Ah, the killer of bees and honey. Have they fallen from being drunk on too much sweet milk?

p- Bitter too. Early and current Pie users go through many trials. It is not an easy road and deliverable only through broken thorns of trust and error. It is hard to verify what one cannot see. But spoken loudly through false prophets is their need for more.

Their motives are empty. They deliver a message of Pie that is incomplete and often pale or black with moralizing morass. That Pie is incorruptible does not make their intent inscrutable. Would that they were not busy filling their bags with false gold.

Delight at discovering Pie is a contagious act, this is true enough. The desire to spread the knowledge and possibility of Pie is mathematically fixed in its code of being. These people seek profit foremost, however. The true essence of Pie is homeostasis, not wealth. May no one save god, or queen, or this mean machine.

P- You can hear it if you listen. Is this why more are not listening?

p- People are not as a whole stupid, but they are tired and weary and done with having the boot placed crafty on their neck while being told they are actually having a good time as they choke down vomit and try to inhale burnt ego scented greed pollution.

P- They are not honest leaders. Nobody is brave enough to tell the truth. Pie's cause is exactly what confuses. Making money is so boring. What the fuck is Pie really and who or what is it good for?

p- Maybe it is to get folks to think about the greed as an act of war, ungreed is bloodless battle and victory all in one. As we are one.

P- Well, that might be well and done in private but to appeal to the masses you need the bits to turn into bobs and oh shit, too many bobs start to bobble and before you know it you are in the black hole of corporations are really people and deserve to vote and of course here to make your life better and oh yeah, wouldn't you too like to be one of great power and wealth through the clean living of Pie? The reason they detract is they are the same sorts of people that brought us this kingdom of hell to begin. They appear as the same trusty takers, all shiny and vapid, as before Pie. These are uninspiring humans on the verge of sick greed virus or fully infected. We are after Pie. Now we see them in the proximity of Pie, speaking loudly for Pie and they should do better. And don't forget the myth that Pie is dirty and bad for the planet. Right?

p- Many myths make many moments of truth telling inevitable. All Pie myths rely on intellectual ineptitude and bad faith arguments supporting overlord overt messages of greed is good.

Instead, they split and send out clown spitters to spread clowning commentary that daring to think there is something better than what they have been selling is unreachable. To think past it all far enough that you see Pie clearly for what it is, a way past them by going through them. Yet, Pie is a promise too great relied on without them. They will not let go easily. You can't possibly have independence and form a new way, new systems, of living. Can I?

P- Silly rabbit, don't you know you need them to keep going?

p- It might seem safer to appeal to pride but this is part of the trap of the system writ large. Tell everyone to look out for themselves whilst having nobody behind you in case you fall. Better pray you do not fall.

P- When it is your fault, if it is your fault, too late, no second, third, fourth chance for you. How many times does it take to succeed?

p- Is that what the Pie hole mascots are trying to sell you and me?

P- It is what they tell themselves. Hard work will set you free and all the remains. They want to win a lot but give you a Pie crumb of imparted wisdom to feel less bad about all their winning and big bags of Pie. They are not smarter. Luck is real. Is it their voice?

p- They're crushing that fucking Pie. It belongs in a cardboard box tied with string. Carefully carried so as to not get crushed on its way to your neighbor's house to eat, reflect, and have some afternoon tea.

The cacophony of their voice-es is as pleasant as a walrus in pain pretending it is off to perform in the ballet of life.

P- What do you want to be when you grow up?

p- We. We're to start asking our children- When you grow up, do you want to run or work for a corporation. There aren't any other alternatives anymore. Every job goes back to a corporate entity.

P- Bits
Bobbles
Black holes
Bitches don't need another hitcher in the system designed to keep us in line to serve them. Stop being their slave. Or what?

p- Nice. Freedom is not being forced to do things you don't have a choice of.

P- Mean. How is this the system that we're living under?

p- Because we live in a failed state. If they have it their way, those with great power and wealth will have everything and we will have nothing. Where they get things wrong is that their wealth will cease to grow if we are all dead. Or if we find another way of doing things. We will create and live in a state of harmony, or we can live in a state of fear and desperation.

P- Speak to people's-
Pain.
The power they have.
Paint them a picture of future progress. What does the new color smell like or sound like? Taste like? Feel like?

p- Like breakfast in bed or a zeitgeber- a stimulus providing event that will test and set and reset an organism's clock. Ticky tack with cues that keep all organisms functioning on a regular schedule. It tastes like a no work weekend morning, with syrup.

P- Bad fetish medicine is the rich telling the poor how to be rich or better yet, how to be better poor. Greed guillotine time?

p- But the economy and capitalism are so good.

P- That statement combines ignorance and arrogance and a looking down their nose at you with the presumption that you are wrong for experiencing your reality?

p- To date, to see in the Pie imaginary, a better world for all, not just a few. Where the few don't exist anymore because we said no in unison.

We agree on much. We are much the same. On this, the elimination of the parasite greed, a harmony is a new color.

P- Theology of conquest-
Faithless.
Mountainous mandates.
A poignant epistle from asshole to assholes.
Is Pie reformation?

p- Reformation is for those holding or needing to be held back. Like a dumb nut too rot to crack. Not yet ripe to be eaten, yet. Just wait. We gonna eat some good Pie off of you. They'll never ever.

Or we take a trip to avoid seven evils and a mountain-
Greed
Cruelty
Religion
Capitalism
Misogyny
Racism
Bigotry
Or
Family
Religion
Education
Media
Entertainment
Business
Government
Or
Ego
Ego
Ego
Ego
Ego
Ego
Ego

Or

I gotta go to the bathroom, are we there yet, can I have some Pie?

P- In any particular order?

p- Mountainous mandates are big and unwieldy. You know?

P- Right. And?

p- Fucking personal and evil. Pie. Politics. Money. Policy. All fucking personal, yeah.

P- Great. So, be personally offended by evil for it is the only sane thing to do, lest they drive me crazy, too. And?

p- The truth of something requires looking at its good and bad parts. That's why the biggest bias in media is story selection. The hateful choir are oxygen thieves. There are not two sides to reality.

P- Many of the greedy tricksters, intent on taking more, are just Pie lickers for themselves, in the business of setting up businesses to do just that, trick you out of Pie, Pie in the mind's eye. And?

p- Cosmic treasures, like math, but unlike earth's resources, never running out. We don't need to envy people anymore.

36

P- *Are you waking up unable to breathe? Is there a tightness in your chest? Are you crying all the time? Does it hurt to look at your children? Do you feel alone and unsure? Do you wonder if there is a future worth living for? Is anyone going to tell the truth?*

You, and we, are not well. You, and we, are going through societal burnout. We are overwhelmed by a cyclone of intensifying social, political, and environmental challenges. We are overwhelmed by the assholes in positions of power and influence who, refuse to rise to the occasion, and instead encourage us to blame each other for our anxiety and discomfort. You are right to be tired and afraid. Oh, but why, oh why?

p- And how.

Unyielding demands of energy, strength and resources, cause us to become weak and fragile until one day we are unable to get up. Technology, information, and unsettled change has brought more challenge than comfort, more dis ease than health. We were never taught to read and write proper because they want to keep us dumb. Along came the long arm of a technological thumb and we are dumber than dumb but plugged up and in like a warm coated bum. We are burnt-out just when things are about to go faster still.

P- Do you feel discarded and invisible?

p- Are dry mouth and a raging impulse to rage keeping you up at night?

P- It is shockingly clear that the shock of the new is over. As such, our feelings have indeed become facts for those unable to cope with a seemingly complex reality but one that is really quite easy to see and absorb if only one has the literacy and critical thinking skills to tell corporate consenting sensual subjugation from a beer.
When one can't cope, how many flavors of acid punch are there?

p- Why there are two. Corporate kleptocracy and dirt road reality.

P- Other than learning good and reading them good old-fashioned books, especially the ones they are trying to ban, what might one do to prepare for this technological onslaught we face ahead?

p- So we don't all go mad, or madder from the more more gaslighting mind control? To do the impossible loaded with salt.

P- Creative endeavorment, go for it. Call on leaders, become a leader. Bring people together, don't exacerbate division. Are you forgotten and abandoned?

p- Why yes, yes we are.

P- Of course you are?

p- That we as a society have failed in this effort has been shockingly clear for decades if not centuries. Anger, frustration, hopelessness, these are all symptoms of a dying greed nation.

We don't have to answer to or explain to bullies what we know to be true. The social contract has been broken with our leaders. It is time for us to lead ourselves. We manifest this in our hearts and heads by learning about Pie or for those not ready to do the work, Pie adjacent right thinking. There is a wrong and a right way to act properly kind. All one needs to do to get on the Pie train is to be open minded to its presence and potential for powerful, unyielding, substantive change. Our only limitation is not trying. For those too beat down or, for whatever reason, unable to work Pie physically into being, we got you. Now, think of that new color.

P- There are many pieces in a great pie, always better shared. Pie is not a solo affair?

p- Abusers never stop until they are made to. As we tragically gaze upon glazed over souls, many victims require the input of many hands, heads, and hearts.

P- Pie may seem immaculately conceived but now that confection is here, we need to raise it together. Is there leavening in Pie?

p- Not traditionally.

P- New color, new traditions. That piece of the Pie is our next step. A deep thank you goes out to all that propelled Pie to this level. There is more work to do. Stop trusting elders?

p- Old greed sick bullies and dictators. In corrupt democracies, they assume positions of power and dominance anywhere they think power can multiply and grow. Pathetic lackeys of power are none too happy to suck the teat of their master. These jerks cling to pure fantasy. They think they are getting closer to being one of them. Still others, longing for a quality of parenting they never received, become fiercely devoted followers of greed and the baby way of crying for more. In a cult, everyone is exactly right.

Eliminating greed whilst battling burnout requires recognition of a link between personal development and trustworthy leadership. We need good leaders, us. At the core of trustworthy leadership is love. Compassion, empathy and dignity make it so. Old is tired.

37

P- Why are some people considered more valuable than others, especially when those currently at the top also get away with doing a lot of harm to those on the bottom?

p- Human currency is a value under siege by individual value perceptions. Change your view, change your mind, change the landscape of being. When how the magic trick is done, is revealed it no longer works. It is just a sleight of hand. Today, they use a sledgehammer. It's a matter of seeing the tool they're using and taking it from them. This does not require anything complicated. A fantasy land where value is malleable and moved at their will is neutralized when Pie is the chosen resource instead of their latest distractions. You are more than all of them, don't look away.

P- Whenever talking about what Pie gets you, use resources not money or wealth, understand?

p- The greed afflicted have only one position- shame, blame, obfuscate, and hide the fact that they are taking our resources.

P- It is more normal not to take more than your share, actually to help those you love and care for before you help yourself, is the human standard. Current positioning and trajectory of greed is not only not good, but also not normal. Not real. It is a projection of self over others. If they want to keep getting away being greedy selfish fucks, they need to convince others to do the same, so they don't look selfish and unfair. We have moved beyond historical norms of greedy assholes pilfering a bit here and there to taking the whole of anything all for themselves. They want the whole damn thing be it mineral, plant, or animal. Use your tools. Use all the tools. You know the ones we're talking about. You have got this.

No biological species or system survives if they eat their young. The walls of a damn will break if it is filled over capacity with liquid greed. It is inevitable, yet illogical. Their pathologies bely a timeline of magnificent self-implosion on the horizon. Why do they do this then?

p- A polemicist pointing out squirrels makes for a bad mate.

Increase use of labor and direct action. We dismantle the system by rejecting it with our bodies and minds. Refuse the refuse.

P- How do we build agency for people?

p- The future is made out of the actions that we take. Make action.

P- We can have nice things. There is so much money around, it just happens to all be stuffed down the pie holes of the greed sick sucks. There are actually not that many of them, a few thousand at best. Imagine life without them in it. What is this shit instead?

p- I am trying to make the revolution irresistible.

Make a beautiful tomorrow. That could be your life. Anybody that resists this is simply trying to steal your hard work's life. They have an investment in maintaining the status quo. They want to continue to take all toys and pleasures. There is something incredibly broken about persons that take zero pleasure in somebody else feeling good. As if your gain means they lose.

Hard work should be rewarded. Money comes from your work. Versus return on work phrasing. We're not idiots, of course our labor is a resource. Our labor is time. Of course, our time is a resource. Pie is return of time, an exponential return of resources.

P- They must be so smart. What do they do with the excess?

p- Greed. And lies about greed. And lies about doing things like research with that money instead of pocketing it all for themselves and their crony buddies. That does not make them intelligent.

P- Couldn't those funds be put to workplace safety, childcare, continuing education, helping the community?

p- If only stupid greed wasn't in the way.

P- Why do we listen to them?

p- Why do we follow fools?

P- Pie is the destroyer of fools?

p- When faced with new information, if we refuse to change, we become their fools for fodder and slaughter because nothing will ever change.

These are not the rules we were told or the way it was supposed to work. What we learned in kindergarten should have been enough. But then the lies begin and never end.

We're all gonna die. Not in the oh yes, ultimately, we are all going to die kind of way. No, as in the they are actively trying to kill us kind of way. At the very least, they want to bring us as close to the brink of death as they can while still wringing our bodies, minds, and souls for profit.

P- Not satisfied with attacking and scapegoating the weakest members of society, in part because their scheme is not working like it once was as more and more know of their evil plan to own it all, they are now going after those in the middle or the managerial class. No one is safe, not even those with matching white collars. Right?

p- Here's the thing. I'm going to the ending of this here right now. This blame ladder has no top rung. They will always, as sure as they are sick puppy kicking greedy fuckers, always chose profit over people over even the damn planet. Fucking unbelievable.

P- We are wrapped in poison bubble wrap?

p- Don't apologize for being decent.

38

P- It is doctrine to the sane looking leaders to encourage only the most limited ineffective resistance to mobilized greed lest the people's passions grow into an event spelling the end of mass greed. They too are on the take. Sustained mass ungreed energy threatens their existence.

Pie is like handing the many dying of thirst a boat full of water and telling you to take just one thimble full and definitely do not tow it down the shore telling neighbors and friends water is near.

They would rather hand power over completely to those with great power and wealth than mobilize the people. They can't risk a spark turning into a fire against those with great power and wealth because they are them and the jig will be up. Something that questions the privileges of the whole system is antithetical to their modus operandi. Use your invisibility to disappear them loud.

But this is the natural result of unnatural greed. Sacrifice everything good and everyone decent for the rabid greed parasite. Any aberrance, a little bit of more more thinking, soon metastasizes if left unremoved. I know you can be clever like a good not evil greed fox. I know you have mad skill power sets they cannot see coming because they have no vision, just pain.

What's the point at which no is not a question?

p- What is the tally of murdered souls we opt out to opt into?

P- To birth an alternative system over this nightmare?

p- We are what we think. All that we are arises. With our thoughts. With our thoughts, we make our world. Said no one or buddha working in private equity. Brouhaha.

P- Pie is a handbook. It tells you what to do. Still tired?

p- Shuffle past bullies in a graveyard. Yes, very.

They're not givers, they're takers who've tricked us into calling each other takers. We are the givers and the makers, and the bakers and they need to be shut up, locked up, made to go away.

P- What we pay attention to grows. Not in admiration but in energy. This is why the more we are self-focused to a point of clinical obsession, we are more unhappy, disconnected, and weaker as a society. Expand beyond the notion of helping self over others. And?

p- And they help themselves to all our resources and then they tell us to fight each other over scraps. This is personal.

P- Is this an unserious land?

p- *Enervate* is a choice word to describe a situation in which someone or something is really fucking tired and lacks vitality, or strength. The verb is most common in the forms *enervated* and *enervating*, as in greed babies *enervated* by a fair not free market on a summer afternoon and a tedious discussion on how to eradicate greed is completely *enervating.* Sweet grapes.

P- If we are free, why are we not able to opt out of this supposedly free system of profit for one of peace and communal governance?

p- Permissions.
Indulgences.
Because they're just too damn greedy.
You cannot be neutral, for neutrality benefits those with great power and wealth. Oh yeah, you will never be one of them.
It is not inevitable. We have been trained to think the problem too big, too ingrained that we just have to live and accept things the way they are. Bullshit. They've got us beaten down and bruised. It doesn't have to be this way. It's not working. It's not ok.

P- Pie is private peace. You can mourn the time they stole from you in private. I don't know about you, but they stole a lot of time, and time is not forgiving. Learn, laugh, lampoon the enemy.

It is not inevitable. We have been trained to think the problem too big, too ingrained that we just have to live and accept things the way they are. Bullshit. They've got us beaten down and bruised. It doesn't have to be this way. What else?

p- Money turns you into an asshole. We treat those without great power and wealth not great. Not great at all. It is for this reason that so many trying to climb that rope to more more money and things and status become such assholes. Seeing how we treat those without means, so mean and gross, is a warning- don't fall down, they'll be no one to help pick you up. Be sure to walk over that human person downtrodden and hurt for if you look down it may just be you someday and oh well for you.

Also, be sure not to get shot while you ignore those in pain and struggling. Wouldn't want to bother the abusers to send thoughts and prayers while they're busy being the opposite of godly and pure. The self-righteousness that follows these evil doers is astounding. Fuck these fucking fuck fuckers all fucking time.

It's almost as if the devil pushed them up to play sick games of sin and purgatory on this here beautiful earth. Hypocrisy is so boring. Time to stroke and rub my ammo and be tough like.

39

P- What is a thing to say in departing?
p- It's not ok.
It's not ok.
It's not ok.
It's not ok.
It's not ok.
It's not ok.

It’s not ok.
It’s not ok.
It’s not ok.
It’s not ok.
It’s not ok.
It’s not ok.
It’s not ok.
It’s not ok.
It’s not ok.
It’s not ok.
It’s not ok.
It’s not ok.
It’s not ok.
It’s not ok.
It’s not ok.

It doesn’t have to be this way.

P- Said the people who take their shower at the end of the day?

p- Yeah. We should really listen to them.

40

P- Freedom is not fathomed?

p- I fathom; therefore I know the reason we exist or occur. You cannot prove otherwise.

P- There must be a shift in Pie consciousness. A real shift in how we think and do, or don’t do. Starting with what our priorities are as people. Those that must focus on food and shelter, those dying on streets in despair, those unable (no we are not going to means test why they’re unable)- we do this work for them because of them. Because if we were in such a situation, for whatever reason, we would want someone to give a helping hand. And it’s the decent good fucking right proper thing to do. Innit?

p- The good news is that the world hasn't gone crazy. You are not crazy. A few thousand evil sick assholes are ruining the celestial party for all of us. And really, just as they intimidate us by trying to silence us, there's only a few of these greed fuckers we need to quiet, disable, dismantle their serfdom doing to send the message we are done being stepped over and stepped on.

Shame tum time. Does their stomach ache?
There you go.

41

P- These are not smart people, destroying the planet and thinking we'll just move to another fucking planet when this one becomes uninhabitable. These are weak ass idiots. They light their farts on fire thinking it is funny, won't hurt too bad, and I'll just buy another couch if I ruin this one. Then this stupid jerk's house is on fire and the complete jackoff idiot just moves to a different house, maybe even a mansion this time. Fucker. That's just gonna be more kindle for the flames. More fire, move, more fire, oh shit. Now the block, town, city, state, country, continent, planet is on fire. Oops. What fucking dumb weak ass fuckers these jerkoffs are. Me me and mine mine selfish ass fuck fuckers. Fucking, fuck them all. Don't look in the mirror now because I am you now?

p- Nice to see all that color. Ok, but let's call them geniuses and idolize them instead. Don't be an idiot too. Two losers don't make a winner. Just more people that shouldn't be anywhere near the decisions that affect our lives. You want to light your ass on fire, have at it but do it in a pit far away from people, plants, and animals. Fucking no good greed feeding virus spreading losers. Don't be an idiot, don't idolize idiots destroying everything good.

P- If you take care of the least among us, you will have a better safer society and a more prosperous future for everyone?

p- What, am I an asshole now, too? Of course billionaires should not exist. These are not trick questions.

P- Ignore bleached reefs, a rising tide lifts all boats?

p- We cannot lose our humanity in the pursuit of humanity. Inclusion vs. malice and division help the seas and the lands.

P- Ok, greed nation is not about the nation but about greed power. What happens to the people who don't believe this stuff?

p- Faith at its core is about love, truth, and justice. If we did that right, what a place we would know.

Told over and over again that we are in danger. That you need to fight if you don't want to lose your country. Greed as a means to an end. The end being authoritarian. Fight for your very own noose said the fat goose to the flock of sheeples. Yep, I saw that.

P- If you don't grow up in a pluralistic society, town, family, you are going to have a narrower view of difference as possibility and strength, not danger. Your version of a public square and how we all come together is limited. Evil selfish forces will prey on that lack of exposure and turn the other into an enemy, simply because it serves their lust for power and greed. It's a bit like taste. If all you've ever had is apple pie you will never know how many different and delicious other flavors of pie are out there. For those afflicted with the evil greed virus to take advantage of you and other sheltered vulnerable individuals and communities you must be unarmed with intelligence and awareness of what is beyond your door, field, nation, book of faith. The same goes with money. The current system and the way it is is fine for the those with great power and wealth because they get all the benefits. Don't buy it?

p- Of course there is another way otherwise they would not be telling you to enjoy the loose lies they serve. Of course we know this way is killing us, seems if we don't get tight there is no good outcome for us plebeians. A rust belt land in greed nation gets that way from too much greed and lead infected water snake holes.

P- So simple and obvious but our heads are in the sand from too much pressure. You are not safe. Society is not safe. The reassurance does not exist out here. The equilibrium humans thought we were working, striving towards is a fantasy. If this was always the plan, then we have lost. Pie asks you to imagine a different way forward. To scrap everything we thought we knew about money, commerce, labor, and value and to start the clock in reverse. Tick tock, next block is an accumulation of time not a substitute or subtraction of our energy that is time.

Those that seek to divide us will never unite us. Those whose paychecks are dependent on not understanding, will never tell us the truth. When you're accustomed to privilege, equality feels like oppression. Good artists feel, great artists heal?

p- Not you or me alone.

Ring the alarm. Don't be timid or embarrassed. Likewise stand firm not as a bully like them but as an example with a charge worth delivering wrapped in grace and faith in humanity. We were never the enemy, they are. Empathy is hard on the greed sick.

P- How do you know who is an anti-hero?

p- Whoever is at the top. Anyone whose net monetary worth is at a billion dollars or more. We can and will go lower but for the sake of ease and because really there are only a few thousand of these fucking fuckers out there to start, let's work with that figure. All of them should not exist. Their enablers in business, religion, media, and academia should not exist either. They are a pox on our house of humanity and as such need to be treated like the plague they are. Dear oh dear leader, who shall be first to go, no.

P- Can those with great power and wealth also be called weak and without courage?

p- Of course they fall heavy on the cross for great power and wealth and let's add cruelty to their mandates and of course there's no arguing or rationalizing with a non-believer, stay far from them. Dismiss, lie, deny, deflect, destroy, the big not so secret ploy to own it all, rule it all. Freedom then, is being a subject subjugated to their will at will as they cheat, rape, steal, murder, and all the juicy bits, limp dry insecure sick fuck greed infected losers in love with imperialistic wet dreams doth covet and molest.

Not levity but not the gallows.

The least we can do is laugh on the way to the crematorium.

42

P- Greed nation is a mean nation. Let us not live there anymore. The people are hard from pretending. It is harder to lie than to tell the truth. Wearing a mask haggard face. Lack of sunlight and warmth. Let us live over here now.

Our policies produced greed nation. The people in power, our so called leaders, are just pawns for the greed infected. Bought and paid for soulless whores for greedy sick corporations, no offense to whores. And again, corporations are not people no matter what the compromised, corrupt, complicit courts rule. Down with acid rain.

This is a pandemic and in pandemics a lot of people die. So I was told to accept whilst wiping my ass with a coffee filter because you know supply chain stuff while they made off with relief money relieved from all of us essential working no bodies over here. Pursuit of an ethno-nationalist colonial state is part of the end game/ not a game. Keep enough so called enemies around to torture and imprison literally and metaphorically to somehow show that you are a big bad boss when really you are a weak insecure pansy of a monster in person form to continue to trick, deceive, and distract. But we see you, you ol' greedy fuck. We are coming for you. Say and do it in creative essential ways to those with great power and wealth. I know you have it in you, beautiful you.

How do you metaphorically break the greed knees of billionaires?

p- You destroy the source of their power. You destroy the poisonous money with a new way of thinking and doing around round concepts of value and labor. Pie removes the inflationary element of the current system with a deflationary element.

P- Sit down and die in silence?

p- If you start telling people the only way to make them feel safe is to take away rights, you are a liar. Your motives are immediately on the table because you already have power and wealth and now you want to dismiss the small remaining bit of power that the masses have in using their bodies and voice to protest and protect what they have claim to, as good and valuable citizens, express, stand up for, and believe in. Do I look like a pawn? Check mate.

P- How're you doing?

p- I am not ready yet.

P- Joining Pie is like becoming a member of a union. You are joining something bigger than yourself and with that comes responsibility. Pie units are divisible. Pie is transparent?

p- You hurt, I hurt. Children being abused, spouses being beaten, the elderly being taken advantage of, stranger danger went too far. Strangers are still our kin, neighbors, and allies. Evil isn't banal. They wanna get in my mountain, I'm gonna get up in theirs.

P- You ok?

p- These greed sick sucker virus fuckers can't run a company without compassion they certainly are not running greed nation with compassion. They are incompetent leaders.

Greed nation and gaslight nation had a baby.

P- What is it called?

p- Lily pad land where wombs are property not cocoons.

P- Or?

p- Property of the state until born, on your fucking own after that.

P- Or?

p- Freedumb land. They made us stupid on purpose. Read a book.

The way they lie. Or how loud they lie does not make what they are saying any truer. They are just clever liars using proven propaganda techniques to pull the wool over our eyes and ears. Don't believe your lying eyes.

P- It exposes the poverty of the greed argument?

p- You can't win an information war unless you admit that we're in one. Stop treating this like it is some natural disaster. We are all the targets of this. Disinformation has three goals. One is to get you to believe a falsehood. The second is to be polarized around that falsehood and to distrust the people who don't believe the same thing. The third is to make you feel cynical, to make you feel helpless. That is exactly what a fascist wants you to do.

Now is not the time to give up. Now is the time for direct unrelenting action. You are better at this than you even know. Nobody sees you coming. They think they can get away with this.

P- I don't want to talk about what you believe but why you believe it. Time for one more waking nightmare. Is that the truth?

p- When you lie to somebody constantly, the consequence is not that they believe the lie, it's that they stop believing anything. They give up their faculty for critical thinking, for questioning. And people like that, you can do anything that you want to them. That's the real danger of the moment that we're in. It's not that somebody is going to take a falsehood for true, or even the truth for a falsity. It's that they're going to give up on the notion of truth and falsity. They're going to start to think that it's indeterminable. If there's no such thing as falsehood, then there's no such thing as blame. There's no such thing as accountability. That is exactly what the fascist wants, giving up on the concept of truth. The fairest on the wall is the least greedy, that is easy to see.

P- Is that the truth?

p- The progenitors of greed nation are the danger. The call is coming from inside the house. Why the fuck would we listen?

P- A healthy, well society cannot be overtaken by a symptom so quickly unless it's nervous system was already beaten down. We were already vulnerable to the greed sot precisely because the system was designed to prosper and slather with prosperity only a few while the rest of us not, in the land of rot. The difference now is twofold. One is Pie, we've never had an exit ramp from money and greed. Two is information, we've never had so much, all at once, good information and bad information at our fingertips.

Whether it's convenience, contagion, or good ol' confirmation bias, we are only as able as the contagion we run from. Run fast.
This the truth?

p- What's the difference?

P- Does it matter?

p- We're all gonna die?

P- Yep.

Neoliberal redistribution has allowed the obscenely wealthy to plunder everything in sight and plug their favorite puppets into every waiting spot, all of it to undermine federal regulation and continue their aggressive takeover. The system has always favored these people. It was founded explicitly to create a system that served the interests of greed sick virus infected fucks, the processes of election and appointment, and even the balance of powers, done to carry out exactly what's been happening ad nauseum. Are you nauseous?

p- Only when my eyes are open. You know, like awake.

P- A healthy society, supported by a healthy system, would not crumble quickly from the pouted shouts of a culled populace.

To address this crisis, it is going to take a sea change the likes of which it is almost impossible to comprehend. It's like asking the blind to imagine a color they have never seen before. This is because we have been taught, in our history, in our politics, in the very reality that is thrust upon us, that we have been living in the end of history and that we are incapable of change. It will need to be personal, cultural, political, spiritual, and it will require so much individual and collective work that it is hard to communicate effectively. This system and this culture are sick. Get it get it?

p- They don't have this under control.

P- Or, rather, they do. And their goals aren't what you're being told. A larger plan to own it all. A plan that is the culmination of a half century of machinations by those with great power and wealth and of course, corporations. Our leaders are not serious people. They sell what they were bought to do. Because the consensus, for the last forty years, has been a hierarchical, pro-business, anti-democratic consensus. Voting is performative. Unless that vote is Pie. Time for pie?

p- La la la la la, I can't hear you telling me not to think of a pink elephant, a small orange coin, or an entirely new color solution to this problem. Here is what I hear- join Pie vs. have our own Pie. An idea shouldn't be owned, like land or love or rights. We are the patriots.

If there is no room to decry greed now, it is going to be illegal, near impossible if greed nation gets to grow more. They break legislation to then argue the legislative process is broken. Gaslight us a little more, my eyes and ears and whatever are only bleeding a little bit. If you break the cycle, you end the fist.

P- It is up or down. For decades, the money has moved from the bottom up. There is wealth redistribution from poor people to not poor people, with the highest concentration going to the least poor. Guess those with great power and wealth are really just socialists and communists for the rich. Don't project onto me your insane pathetic pathological more more. They love that welfare for thee.

Here I go laughing at the hypocrisy only to be interrupted by all the crying about the futility of a fit future because no one tells the truth anymore, there are no more heroes. It's just fucking us. Holy shit. We are all going to die?

p- That was you laughing? Yes. We are all gonna die. That terror comes with a side of liberation, you know?

P- Things can always get worse. Maybe they make insurance forms more complicated and means testing meaner?

p- When are we going to take the gloves off, when there's nothing left to fight?

P- I know your life is hard. It's all getting harder all the time. People do care about people and the everyday problems we face. But we are ignored. We are silenced. Pie is a voice. It speaks in ways that cannot be ignored and is too late to be silenced. Shut up their greed money and change the system. Pie is a vote.

It has to be more thorough than anything we've ever done before.
Our previous tries didn't stick.
Almost there?
And?

p- Accumulate more more capital and greed nation is a nation of laws- this is supposed to be what motivates and guides us? Really really, that is some bullshit.

P- We're all gonna die?

p- Now you've got it.

Ungreed Now

There was an old greedy fucker that swallowed a shoe.
They started to turn blue.
And not knowing what to do.
At first, we stared.
Then we thought.
Then we haught.
And taught.
And laughed.
Absofuckinglutely, the thing to do.
That old greedy fucker was quite dark blue by now.
No matter.
Cause we caught.
Against naught.
We ought some Pie.
Thank you, old greedy fucker.
Now we know what to do.

About EATMS Productions

What's happening to women now is not random. It's structural.

Policy, culture, technology, and power are moving in the same direction.

EATMS maps them clearly and shows how to respond.

This title is part of an ongoing body of work. All EATMS Productions titles, across all series, authors, and formats, are components of a single connected project.

Start here: EATMS System Primer — Free Bundle
https://eatms.gumroad.com/l/dyvzbw

For full catalog or inquiries: eatms.me

Free survival booklet + EATMS updates: email "EATMS" to eatms@pm.me

Please feel free to burn part or all of this book, safely, as an effigy.

www.ingramcontent.com/pod-product-compliance
Lightning Source LLC
LaVergne TN
LVHW050959080826
845145LV00009B/2367

* 9 7 8 1 9 6 6 0 1 4 0 3 4 *